FREE TO SOAR

My Journey
Out of Abuse to Freedom

By
Rebecca Adams

DEDICATION

This book is dedicated to every staff member and volunteer of a domestic violence shelter, both past and present; each one of you is a hero to me! Many untold success stories, as well as my own, would not be possible without your willingness to serve the men and women who have found themselves in a time of crisis. From the bottom of my heart, thank you. Truly, countless lives have been spared due to your tireless efforts. I salute you. As you carry on your difficult work, please know you are *deeply* appreciated.

A NOTE TO THE READER

There is a reason this book has found its way into your hands. If you discover that its contents do not address a need in your life, please give it to someone who might benefit from it. Thank you, as this simple act might save at least one life.

> Gratefully yours,
> Rebecca Adams

ACKNOWLEDGMENTS

First and foremost, I want to give all thanks to my Father for walking through every moment of this difficult life with me, then for helping me relive it as I wrote this book. Thank You, God, for your faithfulness!

Mom, even though probably never read this, I want to thank you. I would not be who I am today if it was not for your example. I love you and I'm so very proud of you. You were my hero. For all you lived through in your hard life, you continued to push through each difficulty with strong determination. The tenacity you modeled is both inspiring and a source of strength. You were awesome!

I am blissfully proud of my two sons, my other two heroes. Thanks to your support, counsel, and helping hands, I was able to leave and get a brand-new lease on life. I will be forever grateful. I don't think I could have done it without your help. You amaze me at how you've become such uniquely wonderful men. Even though you may not like it, just deal with the fact that I will never stop saying how proud I am of you. For your support with this book, I am unceasingly grateful. I love both of you so very much.

Even as I thought about what to write to my pastor and his wife, I began to choke up. The two of you have allowed me to truly be myself in the years I've known you. You loved me when I was putting walls up, was acting weird, cantankerous, and you couldn't figure me out. Yet you continued to love me. How does one ever truly say a sincere thank you for that? You have been "Jesus with skin on" for me and many, many others. (Yes, I was crying as I wrote this.)

For the pastor from the town I grew up in, I am equally choked up thinking about all you've done. You were there in an instant when it was time to get my daughter out of an abusive situation. More times than I will ever be able to remember you were there to receive a phone call from me while I sobbed on the other end, hours away, while I was missing my family and trying to make sense of my new life as it was taking shape. Your home has always been open to all who need you. To say thank you is not sufficient, but it is truly sincere. (Yep, I cried here, too.)

To all the precious friends who prayed with me before I left my abusive (now ex) husband, thank you. For your unceasing support through the years, I have no English words to describe how precious you are to me. Our friendships were simply enriched and deepened by the tough times. Thank you from the bottom of my heart. You will always be sisters and brothers in my heart.

To my precious co-workers, thank you so much for being such enthusiastic cheerleaders with this project. We are truly family, mixed nuts, Lemon Sisters and all! Joan W., do you know this book may never have been written without your encouragement? How do I thank you for that? Christine, you did a *beautiful* job as my editor! Thank you for the time, work, and expertise you put into this.

Tammy, as my Project Manager, you deserve a medal for your patience! Thank you for all you did.

For the WinePress staff (my original publisher), you were wonderful! Thank you so much for the grace you showed with my repeated need for extensions to get this done with excellence. You have been such fantastic professionals to work with! I cannot thank each of you enough.

To Russ, who has added to his white hair by doing edits, edits, and more edits to assist me in getting my book formatted and uploaded to my third publisher in e-book, audio, and the second edition print – the two words of thank you sound so trivial and insincere. Honestly, I don't know what I would have done without you through these huge projects. You are so appreciated! It was great knowing that you and your precious wife, Bev, are so trustworthy. Also, I know that both of you only produce first-rate quality!

Table of Contents

Dedication iii

A note to the Reader v

Acknowledgments vii

Fleeing 1

Chaos 13

Stifle 43

Confusion 57

Twisted 91

Whirlwind 115

Untangling 129

Discoveries 157

Directions 177

Freedom! 199

Renovated 213

Epilogue 227

Breaking It Down 241

   Cyberbullying 246

   Cyberstalking 247

   Financial Abuse 248

   Incest 250

   Isolation 251

Neglect 252

Physical Abuse 253

Psychological Abuse 255

Sexual Abuse 260

Spiritual Abuse 265

Stalking 268

Verbal Abuse 270

Voyeurism.. 273

Additional Resources 275

Endnotes.. 281

FLEEING

You yourselves have seen...how I carried you on eagles' wings and brought you to myself. (Exodus 19:4 NIV)

As I fled from everything I had ever known, loved, and hated, I entered a totally unknown world. Everything was unfamiliar, even the driving I had to do. I never had driven on a long trip before, much less, completely alone. This would be a four-to- six-hour drive. My car had an oil leak. I was so scared. No, I was terrified. Yet I recently read, "Even if you're afraid, do it afraid,"[1,] and God had spoken so clearly to me, saying that was a "now" word for me.

Logic simply could not function in this situation. I was leaving my entire family—my three children, grandson, brother, sisters, and mother. In the thirty-five years, I had lived in this town, I'd known a lot of people. All of the streets and scenery were like old, familiar companions. This had been my home town since I was a child. I would be leaving the dearest friends I ever had known. My fleeing would do more than merely upset a few of them. Only about a dozen people knew my plans. There would be those who didn't know whose very belief in God would be rocked. Knowing that ripped at my heart.

I hugged my eldest son as he left for work, not knowing when I would see him again. We both uttered intense, unspeakable words with our eyes. It all ran far too deep for common, verbal communication. I didn't think my heart could take the profound pain that I was feeling. Yet I knew this was right. I had to leave. I don't remember what we said in the quietness of that kitchen, but I never will forget what our eyes conveyed: *"I love you so much." "Take care of yourself." "I know this is the right thing to do, but I'm so afraid." "Please be careful." "I miss you already!" "Will I ever see you again?" "How far away are you going?" "Will you be okay without me?" "Will I be all right without you?"* A deep love was shared in those precious minutes. When we hugged for the final time, he buried his face in my neck as he so lovingly used to do when he was a little boy. Surely, he couldn't remember that. It used o melt my heart then. It was no different this time. I fell apart, yet tried so hard to be strong.

FLEEING

This precious son was sending me with a cell phone so I could call for help if I needed it. Plus, it would enable him and his sister to communicate with me without knowing where I was going. It was safer this way. Then if they were asked, they could honestly say that they didn't know where I was. My son also had done all he could to both advise and prepare me for what lay ahead. However, neither of us knew what was truly in store for me. In our wildest imaginations, we never could have conjured up anything as amazing as what God did. Only He could walk me through this journey. If I was going to make it, it could only be as I leaned totally on Him. My future was truly His.

Not long after my emotional goodbye to my eldest son, it was time to take my daughter to work and drop my adorable grandson off at the day care—for the last time. My heart was torn in two as my daughter and I talked and cried in my car outside her workplace. We talked as long as we could. Then it was time for a final goodbye to her. We had to keep our emotions in check so as not to disturb my sensitive grandson. As I watched her walk to the building, I wondered if I ever would see her again. Could my heart take all this pain? She didn't turn and look back. This was tearing her up on the inside, too. I pulled my car away in silence, trying not to cry in front of my perceptive grandchild.

As I got closer to the front door of the daycare, I realized that I didn't know if I could do this. This precious little boy was my pride and joy. Grandmothers don't just go off and leave their grandchildren, not knowing if they ever will be able to hold them again, do they? What was I doing? Yet I had to retell myself that, yes, I *had* to do this. It was time.

The babysitter knew the situation, and she acted as though this was a completely ordinary day. I placed my sweet toddler in her capable hands. She, too, had fled from a similar situation and knew what I was going through. She hugged me, reassuring me that she would be praying for me. Having walked more than a mile in my moccasins, she cautioned me to be careful. I was a basket case by this time. I was so relieved that my grandson had run off to play with the other children. It would have upset him too much to see his Nana like that.

FLEEING

With a heavy heart and very heavy feet, I walked away. Would he remember me? He was so young. Less than two years of age is not enough time to build lasting memories of your grandmother, is it? Everything in me wanted to run back inside, change all my plans, stay where I was, and not leave this precious child. Yet the mere thought of the torment that would come if I stayed caused me to see that I needed to keep moving forward. To remain in my current situation was truly unthinkable. It was time to leave. I had to trudge on. It was time to get on with the next stage of all this. Even as I drove home, I tried to be as calm and focused as possible, and I asked the Lord what needed to be accomplished next.

As I arrived home, my youngest son and I began to load my vehicle nervously. I had pulled it into the garage and closed the door so none of the neighbors could witness anything. We were like two flighty birds, pulling various things from different parts of the house. Every once in a while, he and I would exchange agonizing looks that betrayed just how difficult this was for both of us. I wondered if I could do this last step. I knew that my children were at

risk and truly could catch hell for my decision. I agonized over that. Yet they all assured me that they were up to the challenge. Each of them had tried to get me to leave their father several times in the last few years. They had confronted him numerous times, warning him that this day eventually would come. So I knew I had their complete support. To this day, I don't think I could have done it without their backing.
Our final good-byes were done with inexpressible agony. Yet we both tried to encourage each other that we would see one another soon, as he was going to come and live with me. Our feelings ran so deep, our emotions so high. Just as with my eldest son, there were no real words to convey our true thoughts and feelings. Saying nothing yet speaking volumes has such depth at times like that. Our unutterable communications would have to speak for now.

    Could I do this? Was it possible that I really could leave my children, grandson, family, friends, and all I owned behind, save what I could transport in my little vehicle? How do you really know that you've packed enough of your life's belongings to begin your life all over again? Could I possibly have forgotten anything? I asked the Lord one more time if I had all that I needed. I had peace. It was about time to go, so I took my two new bumper stickers off the back of my car so that I would be less recognizable to law enforcement.

Now there was one more thing that needed to be done. I had my son call the man we both considered our pastor and ask him to come to anoint both my vehicle and me with oil before I took off for the last time. As this precious man began to pray, I sensed the rich presence of the Holy Spirit descend and completely fill that grungy little garage. I thought it was all my imagination. But then he stopped in the middle of his sentence and said, "I feel the presence of the Holy Spirit in this place." Countless times in the months ahead as doubts popped into my mind, I would reflect on God's manifest presence as a sign of His blessing and approval of what I was about to do. I was overwhelmed. I was touched to the very core of my spirit. God didn't bless a wife leaving her husband just because he was abusive, did He? Yet I knew He clearly and sovereignly had led me to this point. There were final hugs and wrenching good-byes from these two precious men as I sobbed, and then it was time to leave.

My nerves were high. Shakily, I climbed into my car and began to pull out of the garage. Then I remembered that the oil needed to be checked. One final check showed that I was ready. Slowly, I backed out into the driveway. The only relief besides leaving my abuser was bidding adieux to the back-breaking yard work. I audibly said, "Good riddance, flower beds. I won't miss you." I would miss the money I could make from the fruit grown in our yard, but it wasn't worth staying for. God would provide. Reality set in again. I looked back several more times as I slowly pulled away. There are no words to describe the searing pain in my heart as it was being torn into so many different pieces. I truly did not know if I could live through all this pain. I wept as I drove away.

I now was officially on a road that only God had mapped out. My new life was beginning, and I didn't have a clue what that entailed. My head swam with worries about my unknown future. *How will my family react when*

FLEEING

they find out that I left my husband? What about the people I went to church with? Then there were friends to consider, dear people I truly had come to know and love.

I had to drive through the city, where my husband worked. *Will he see me? Will he send the law after me? How bizarre and horrifyingly ugly could this get?* I honestly couldn't recall ever being this frightened before. He would be so incredibly angry if I were caught. My mind ran the full gamut as to what might take place. I worried about the future. The little bit of money I had would not sustain me for very long at all. *What will I do? Just exactly how far will my money stretch? With an oil leak, how will my vehicle do on such a long drive? What if I need to have my car repaired along the way? How much would it cost? Would I get a trustworthy mechanic? How expensive is it to live in the town I am moving to? Once I get to my destination, where will I stay?*

Shortly before I left, I called a shelter that I had been referred to. The lady I spoke to said they didn't have a place for me to stay. I got uncharacteristically aggressive and explained to her that I couldn't wait. I had to leave right now, while my husband was at work.

She said to just come on anyway. I was headed directly into an unknown future, and I didn't even know if I had a place to sleep that night. Yet every time a panicking thought would rush through my mind, I would stop the entire thought process and dump that worry in the hands of Jesus. I told Him that if I didn't have Him to guide me, I was sunk. Continually, I told God that I desperately needed Him, and I prayed almost unceasingly for wisdom.

Two or three times I stopped and let the car cool off so that I could check the oil. So far, everything looked good. I was so very grateful for the Lord's loving, watchful care over me. I sped on. The four-to-six-hour drive was reduced to less than three hours of actual drive time. I truly believe it was the Lord who prevented me from getting a ticket for speeding.

Faces and names of those who were so very dear to me flashed through my mind, and I wondered what they would think when they found out that I had left. I knew ahead of time that some would side with my husband. With others, it was difficult to determine what their opinions would be. I simply had to lay each person, his or her reaction, and my friendship with him or her before the feet of my precious Jesus. This was the first in a long series of my releasing all sorts of things to the Lord. The emotional anguish was not only indescribable but also a constant companion. To this day, I don't recall another time when I had to lean entirely on God like that.

How in the world had my life gotten to this point of crisis? What possibly could have brought me to this decision that would look so reckless and rash to so many? I believe the story of my upbringing will answer those questions and more.

FREE TO SOAR

CHAOS

If God hadn't been for us when everyone went against us, we would have been swallowed alive by their violent anger, swept away by the flood of rage, drowned in the torrent; we would have lost our lives in the wild, raging water. (Psalm 124:2-5SG)

[My father] articulated his words and moved in such a manner as to control and force us into obedience. My father seemed to enjoy seeing our fearful submission, and if we dared to disobey, our punishments far exceeded our crimes.[2]

~ Shirley Jo Petersen, *The Whisper*

Our father was a strong dictator, and getting his own way was critical for him. His lust for power and prestige were the biggest reasons he remained a minister. For him, the "Reverend" in front of his name was a power trip, as he thrived on the authority it gave him. It helped to fill a hole that was left from the wounds of his childhood. Later, he confided to me that being a pastor was the worst occupation he could have ever pursued. He confessed that the authority it gave him provided opportunities to misuse that power.[3]

~ Shirley Jo Petersen, *The Whisper*

My life began as quite a shock to my parents; my very existence was unplanned, to say the least. My older brother and sister were only twenty-one months apart in age; it was similar to raising twins. Then in the midst of my father's going full-time to seminary, working full-time to support the family, and being the pastor of a small community church, I showed up on the scene. I know I added to the chaos. And if that wasn't enough, for the first year of my life, I was very sick. On two separate occasions, the doctor wasn't even sure I would make it. In my first year of life, I had pneumonia twice, and the measles. If you're not putting two and two together yet, let me just say that tight finances, mounting medical bills, the expense of another mouth to feed and care for, and a new, fussy baby all combined with an overworked father who needed to be able to study and sleep and five people living in a small house was not a good situation. And it didn't help that my father was a very impatient man.

CHAOS

To say things were hairy in our home is more than likely an understatement.

Years later, I found out that my father was physically abusing both my brother and sister. For some reason, I escaped his wrath. Before I was born, my father said that he had ruined the lives of my two siblings, but he was not going to do the same with me. To this day, I don't understand why I eluded his intense anger. It is still a mystery to me, but I am grateful to the Lord for whatever the reason was. Many years later, my father admitted to me that he attempted suicide during this time. I sometimes wonder if it would have been better for all of us if he had been successful.

When I was four years old, my father graduated from seminary. I have a few vivid memories of that, even though I was so very young. I recall that during the ordination we were seated in the balcony with a bird's eye view of my father and all the other men in his class. I watched spellbound as they knelt to be prayed for. Even at that tender age, I knew that this was a solemn moment. That long line of black-suited gentlemen kneeling before the

Lord made quite an impressive sight for this little girl.

I also recall sensing the Holy Spirit hovering in that auditorium. It was the first time I felt what His precious presence is like. Such a rich peace filled that huge place.

Within a year, our lives would change more drastically than any of us possibly could have imagined. And within five years, our family life would be turned completely upside down and ripped apart.

My father had not reacted well to the constant stress of full-time studies, full-time work, a small pastorate, and a family. It had taken him six years to complete college and then another six in seminary when most students finish in four each. Looking back, it's amazing he made it at all. As a man of hair-trigger rage, stress was something my father never learned how to handle. He began to pull away from the Lord. As he did so, his standards gradually were lowered. Approximately one year after his ordination, my father switched to a more liberal denomination to accommodate his new and ever-changing beliefs. It was the

CHAOS

beginning of a spiral downward that seemed to have no end.

Due to his change in churches, a move was inevitable for our storm-tossed family. We moved from a very large city to a rural town with a population of 300. The culture shock was almost more than my parents, brother, and sister could take. I was only five years old when we moved, and I don't recall it being anything traumatic for me. However, I do recall their misery.

In this quaint little town, my brother and sister could walk with me wherever we wanted or needed to go. I even recall occasionally walking home from first grade by myself. The house furnished to us by the church was not in good shape. Just a few years after we moved out, it was torn down.

That pastorate only lasted a year. Then it was on to yet another rural area, where my dad pastored two small churches, just as he had before. Although the parsonage was fairly new and far superior to the last one, a house does not make a home. The occupants decide what it will be like inside those four walls with the choices they make. My father already had begun molding our private home into a place of tension and fear with his frequent bouts of anger. His explosive episodes were now more frequent. It was a really difficult time for all of us. My mother tried to do what she could to bring back the husband she once knew, but he pulled further away and became even more irate. Also, by this time, my father's spiritual downslide had worsened, and yet he seemed to be trying to keep it hidden from us. Did he think we wouldn't notice? Even for this young second-grade girl, the beginning of his metamorphosis was apparent. He was no longer the father I remembered.

One year later, we had to leave that wonderful little town. This was hard for me, as I had become attached to my friends at school and church and was very comfortable in my school. I was enjoying that pretty little place. There seemed to be tranquility there, although it certainly couldn't be found in our house. My delightful piano teacher even lived next door. And with permission, I could walk to the church to see my dad. But all of this was going to change. This was my fifth move in the short eight years of life. Unbeknownst to me, moving was something I would need to become accustomed to.

Our next stop took us to a larger city, where our parsonage was out in the country. It came complete with a flock of fenced-in hens and a chicken coop perched partway up the hill in the field behind the house with a beautiful, soft rabbit in an adjoining room. The house next door to us had a girl who was just one year older than I was. She was outgoing and very active. She took me under her wing, and we became inseparable friends. This was an absolute paradise for me.

My brother and sister did not fare so well. My brother was not accepted at school, and my sister was tormented by her peers because of her weight. Their abuse at home continued. I was told years later that I was always conveniently sent out of the house before anything took place.

Dad's spiritual decline was spiraling downward at a breathtaking pace. I've been told it was while we lived in this house that he decided to permanently replace the family Bible on the coffee table with *Playboy* magazine. Don't ever let anyone lie to you and say that pornography is harmless. We all still suffer the effects of it. I also recall the distasteful programs my dad began to watch on television. As the leader in our home, his choices ushered in all sorts of evil spirits. We had no choice in the matter. It is definitely something I now can look back on and see how our choices directly impact everyone around us. No one can live in an environment like that and escape unscathed.

My "paradise" in this country home lasted the typical one year. My father left the ministry and began a teaching job out of town. It was a drastic change in our lives. Because we had been living in the parsonage, we had to move—yet again. This was move number six in my short nine years. This time, at least we stayed in the same town. In this move, I not only lost a wonderful friend next door but I had to attend a different school, again. Now I was in the fourth grade, and it was my fourth school. At least I could walk the half block to and from school each day. My sister also was able to walk the few blocks to the junior high school. In the midst of all this, my mother did her best to run the house as smoothly as possible. One difficult thing was that we continued to

CHAOS

attend the same church where my father had been the associate pastor.

Dad lived in a boarding house during the week and came home on the weekends. It was a very odd arrangement, but it was probably to keep us in the same school system. This living arrangement also became a convenient cover-up for my father's extramarital affair that he had begun with another teacher at work. His personal life was taking some other new turns as well. I remember the time he brought home a marijuana leaf carefully wrapped in foil to show us. He said that if we ever saw anything like it, we were to bring it to him. By this time, I was very disgusted with the person he was choosing to become. In a smart-aleck tone, I asked him why he wanted us to bring it to him; was it so he could smoke it? He flashed an evil Grinch-like smile and gave a vague response. I knew what the real answer was. He had spoken volumes with that ambiguous reply and evil grin.

When my dad was home, it ranged from very uncomfortable to volatile. He drifted further and further from us emotionally. Also, my mother had begun to work part-time to help pay some of the debt my father had accumulated throughout the years. His level of responsibility was going down the tubes, just like his personal life. He was not even attempting to pay these dear friends and family back the money they had lent him.

We lived in that house for the all-too-familiar length of one year. This time, though, we only moved a few blocks. All three of us were able to stay at the same school for two years in a row. It was unheard of in my short academic life. This felt comforting, yet it seemed we could sense something was about to change again.

Sure enough, over Christmas break, my dad lowered the boom and informed us that he and mom would be getting a divorce. My world fell apart. My grades already had begun to drop, but they took a nose-dive at that point. My mom had reason to be concerned. She could see that I was suffering and that my brother and sister were too. I can't imagine the emotional torment she was enduring.

Since leaving the ministry, my father had had more time to spend with my brother, something he had been lacking. He took my poor brother down the same path he was plummeting down.

My sister was now an emotional wreck. Her abuser was gone now, which was good, but she never had been able to please him with anything she ever had attempted. Her yearning for a loving daddy who would unconditionally accept her never would be realized in him. At best, he seemed to tolerate her existence. I was to learn years later that in essence, he blamed my sister for having been born. But it was his decision the night she was conceived not to use the birth control device that my parents had chosen. The shifting of his anger from himself to my sister was not only poorly placed but also showed further evidence of a sick and immature man.

My father's leaving put my mother in a huge mess. To begin with, she now had to find a full-time job. Her employment meant our survival. It also meant that I was left alone for hours at a time in the evenings. Dad had taken the only TV we owned, so the house was eerily silent during the dark evenings while my brother and sister were out with friends. Even the companionship of our two dogs couldn't replace what this nine-year-old really needed—parental love, guidance, attention, and supervision. I ached inside because of the emotional trauma I had been through. We all did. I had no one to talk to about any of it. I don't believe my mother did either.

One night, the only thing I could think of to pass the time was to get out my crayons and coloring books. As I sat there alone in that dark, quiet, and empty two-story house, my box of colors fell over. It scared me so badly that I jumped and almost knocked over the table where I'd been sitting. When my mom came home from work, I told her what had happened. She decided to buy a small, portable, $99, black and white television to help me pass the time and to create some noise in the otherwise soundless house. But then a new problem arose that neither of us anticipated. I began to anesthetize my pain with this new distraction. I tried to fill the emptiness of my life with the "reality" of the people on the screen. It became an addiction that I struggled with for years. It wasn't long before my brother moved out to live with my dad. This left my mother to mow the grass—not an easy task for a woman. The place we were renting sat at the top of an extremely steep hill. She actually had to lower the mower down the hill by a rope and then pull it back up again. This procedure was repeated until the entire front yard was mowed. There were times I was afraid that my mom would pass out from the exertion of this ordeal. Seeing her having to go through such difficult physical labor really worried me. I blamed my dad for leaving her to do a man's job. His deserting us created some very deep wounds in me, leaving me both angry and frustrated.

    It would be years before I even could begin to deal with the overwhelming emotion of being abandoned. Yet when those rare occasions came when I saw my father, I never was allowed to express any negative reaction to all this. I knew it would invoke his wrath, the results being unpredictable. I did not have any idea how to cope with any of that. The only coping mechanisms I had seen lived out before me by my parents obviously didn't work, as their marriage was now over. It seemed easier at the time to bury my thoughts and feelings. I didn't have an outlet anyway. In our society then, children rarely saw a counselor. An adult only went to counseling if he or she was on the verge of a nervous breakdown.

Not too many months passed, and Mom was able to find a nice house to rent (the eighth in my ten years, if you're counting). I changed schools again. This time I went back to where I had attended two years prior. Our new house was really nice, with two bedrooms, a kitchen, a living room, a garage, and a full-sized basement. There was more peace in our home than I ever remembered, as the raging abuser was no longer under our roof.

My sister, mother, and I had a lot of emotional wounds that needed to be tended to, but there was nothing available to offer those services to us. Needless to say, none of us possessed healthy coping skills or the ability to heal. So, three scarred females and their hormones had squabbles and spats, but life was better.

My mom gave my sister a bedroom to herself. She needed it. She had suffered the brunt of dad's abuse, plus she was now in her teen years, so a private retreat was a necessity. That left one bedroom for my mom and me to share. I loved it. I now had her all to myself.

CHAOS

The sound of her gentle snoring would begin almost as soon as her head hit the pillow, but it didn't bother me. Her presence on the other side of the room was both comforting and reassuring to the very deepest part of my being. It was quite a switch from the last house, where my bedroom had been the enclosed back porch and my companions were the washer and dryer. I had felt vulnerable out there, plus cut off from the rest of the family. I now no longer felt alone.

I don't know where I would be today if it was not for my loving mother. She was my hero. During this tremendously difficult time in her life, I saw her take on tasks I had no idea she was capable of. Mom excelled. She seemed to soar above her circumstances. She became my rock; she seemed so immovable.

Now my sister could walk the half block to the high school. A very sweet family from our new church lived just up the block, and my sister visited them often. Next door to them was a girl I went to school with, so I was able to ride with them each morning and afternoon. And, of course, Mom continued to work forty-plus hours a week to provide for us. Dad never was consistent with child support, but he did make sure he paid just enough so that he could claim us as a tax deduction each year. It took years before I could forgive him for that. I saw how hard it all was on Mom. I was truly beginning to learn just how unfair life can be.

Once in a while, Dad would visit. Seeing him would evoke such intense emotions: anxiety, joy at the prospect of seeing him again; a deep, inner desire of a young girl to have a real "daddy"; hope that I might please him; disgust at seeing the unfamiliar, foul-mouthed pervert he was becoming; a continually growing fear of what mood he would be in from one millisecond to the next; and constant apprehension about saying the wrong thing that could send him into a tirade. I remember one of the times he came by. It was probably to pick me up so I could spend an entire dreaded weekend with him. I was trying to keep it lighthearted and asked if he wanted to come to the back of the house and see our outside dog. We had gotten her when I was very little. What amazed me was how delighted she was to see him. She cowered at the sight of him, but she also showed my dad such amazing, unconditional love. He had abused her all her life, even breaking a very thick broom handle over her back once because she wouldn't stop barking during the night. That memory of her loving reaction to Dad remains vivid to me after all these years.

During the two to three years we lived in that house, my mom began dating. This disturbed me greatly. I just had begun to feel some sense of calm, normalcy, and a level of peace without my father's presence in our home. Now it seemed like the ground beneath my world was quaking yet again. Was nothing ever going to be stable in this life? I did not deal well at all with this change. I vehemently denied that it had anything to do with my being jealous because her attention was off of me and onto someone else. It was years later before I realized that that was exactly the root cause of my fighting this new phase of my mom's life. As a divorced adult, I now clearly see that she was lonely and yearning for companionship, even marriage.

My mom finally stopped dating the first man and began seeing the one whom she eventually would marry. I truly despised him.

He had only one objective in mind. Okay, maybe two. It was obvious he wanted someone to run the everyday functions in his home and someone to share his bed. By the time we were all enduring their stormy dating relationship, my sister had gone to college and my mother and I had moved—again. We lived in that house for about two years. This second man in my mother's life kept breaking up with her and going back to another woman who had the same first name as his deceased wife. It wouldn't be long until they broke up and he was back with Mom.

Intermittently throughout this time, I received phone calls and letters from my father. I froze each time I heard his voice or saw his handwriting on an envelope. I began to see a pattern. I didn't hear from him until he had it in his mind that he wanted to see me, and a "no" on my part would not be acceptable to him. This only intensified my dread. The evil that oozed from the very core of his being was such a total contrast from the caring minister I remembered. By this time, his house was filled with smoke, which hung in a thick fog, and had a strong, silent undertone of perversion. And

CHAOS

just when I thought it couldn't get any worse, his anger intensified. He became even more unpredictable than ever. I didn't dare risk infuriating him by not agreeing to spend time with him or by bringing up anything that even had the possibility of sending him into an instant display of wrath.

My dad had remarried just three months after divorcing my mom. Initially, I had completely rejected his new wife, but I soon grew to love her dearly. I looked forward to seeing her more than my dad when it came time to visit him. One thing I always have been able to say is that my dad had excellent taste when it came to the women he married.

When I visited my dad, it also was a delight to see my brother. I really missed him, but from what I remember, he was rarely there.

During this time, my dad pinned me against a wall more than once, without touching me, with the feigned notion of intensely talking to me. However, his words never seemed to be connected to the body language he was displaying or the filth that I saw in his eyes. These episodes always left me both confused and afraid. One thing I knew for sure was that his eyes were dripping with lust for me. I had seen that gaze directed at other women many times, and it would become a look that was frequently directed at me. I may have been young and naïve, but I was not stupid. I knew what that meant. I also clearly sensed the horrid, thick, evil presence that hovered over the two of us at those times. To say it was oppressive is a mild description of what I felt.

On one visit, my dad attempted to lure me into the bedroom to watch him and his wife in bed. Years later, my mother told me he'd wanted my brother to come in and watch the proceedings in their room. Perversion has no boundaries.

I remember two things very clearly that took place about four years after he left my mom. One was after I refused to jump at the chance to live with him and his wife. He angrily left his house, but he returned later, storming through the front door. He began picking up anything he could find and then angrily heaving it across the room. I never had seen an adult throw a temper tantrum before, much less my father. I was terrified. My stepmom outwardly seemed to remain calm, but there was no way anyone could be caught in that maelstrom and not be affected.

I was an emotional basket case by the time my dad drove me home. On the way, he pushed me for the answer that I indeed would move in with him. The only answer I would give him was that I would pray about it. He thought he was smearing me with an insult by saying I was just like my mother, but I took it as a very high compliment. I certainly didn't desire to pattern my life after his. For him to compare me with a strong anchor of a woman who loved her God was more than a flattering remark. I preferred to follow a peaceful woman than an unstable, angry man.

My dad called back a week or so later, pushing for an affirmative answer. He was enraged when I turned him down. He began his usual verbal garbage to get me to cry. Then he ended the conversation with a very hateful retort that I still remember years later. He took my "no" as a personal rejection, even though it was merely God's way of protecting me from many things, including sexual abuse. I also clearly recall how he boldly informed me that he smoked marijuana. He then offered to get some for me or my friends to try if we ever wanted it. I was completely shocked. At the most, I was fifteen years old.

Right around this time, the FBI began to pursue him. I'm not exactly sure why, but from what I've been able to learn, it was due to suspicions of him dealing drugs and being a pimp. He and his wife fled to another state for several months. It was blissful for me not to have any contact with him during that time. Although I deeply yearned for him to be a true father to me, I did not want the one he had become. When he did return, the visits and phone calls were intermittent, for which I was grateful. However, each time I had a school function, I felt obligated to invite my dad. Sometimes I conveniently never got around to it. Those few incidents were wonderfully peaceful, as I knew he would not be there. I would not have to see or talk to him afterward.

By the time I graduated from high school, dad was openly growing marijuana in his living room and proudly had smut displayed on his walls. He even had a pornographic shower curtain.

CHAOS

Shortly after I turned fifteen, my mom married the man I despised. (This made move number ten for me.) He finally decided on my mother for a wife. My life took a hairpin turn in the road. To add insult to injury, the daughter of my stepfather's former girlfriend was in my high school. Numerous times I caught her casting hateful looks in my direction. Eventually, I found out who her mother was. Everything in me wanted to tell her that I wished with all my heart that he had married her mom instead of mine. But I was too shy to do that.

Mom and I moved into the house that his family had owned for two generations. I didn't even meet my stepbrother or stepsister until the week before the wedding, and that was only to get us partially moved into the house before "the big day."

After my mom and her new husband returned from their honeymoon, my stepsister was supposed to pick me up from where I had been staying to bring me out for an old-fashioned chivaree. But she forgot. No one ever came to get me. At least a half hour *after* the festivities had begun, I received a phone call from my stepsister. She apologized, saying that they had forgotten to come get me. During the entire conversation, there were sounds of laughter in the background. I could hear friends and family having a good time. After I hung up, I sat at home, feeling completely left out. The hurt was too deep to describe. The words "unimportant," "rejected," "abandoned," and "alone" don't even come close. I never felt fully included in his family. That incident, which could have helped form some sort of bond, was merely an indicator of the future.

For five long years, I lived under my stepfather's oppressive roof. I secretly nicknamed him "Hitler." Every time I came around him, I could sense that my hatred of him was reciprocal. The "bad vibes" were intense. He ran his house as though he was a dictator. Words cannot describe how tense and miserable it was. My new house became my prison, with yet another school as the other one. There was no escape from either.

To save on utilities, he did some things I considered extreme. For example, the house did not have air conditioning. As my mother and I would be in the kitchen canning vegetables on a

100-degree day, he would walk in and turn the box fan down from the "high" setting to "low." That scenario was repeated more than once. Yet several years later, after he had major surgery, he was no longer able to tolerate the heat. He immediately bought a window air conditioner so he could be comfortable. It didn't matter that we had suffered for years.

There were other things he did to save on utilities. If supper was being prepared around sunset, he would walk in and turn the light off to save on the electric bill. Then it would be turned back on when he came to sit down for supper. This was a common occurrence. Also, the house never had been insulated, because that would be too costly. During my first winter there, I awoke one morning to see snow on the *inside* of my window sill. The family thought it was funny. They were used to it. I never have seen the humor in that. My mother stuffed rags in the gaps to help make it warmer. Yet I still had to wear my winter coat, hat, and gloves while studying in my room. Since I was so very ill as an infant, I never had been able to tolerate cold temperatures and was susceptible to sickness.

And to make it worse, one night after supper, my stepfather walked into my bedroom without knocking. He did not say a word, but he went directly to the propane stove and turned it down so that it was barely on. He then silently walked out.

There were other issues with the house. For one thing, it was infested with huge spiders. And at night, you often could hear the mice running up and down the walls. One of the buildings on the property had had termites for years. Yet my stepfather never hired an exterminator. That would cost money.

My stepfather was very controlling of my mom. Although this house had more than ten rooms, my mom was given only the 6' x 8' utility room to decorate however she wanted. The rest of the house was left as he wanted it. It remained that way until his death and Mom moved into a nursing home following a stroke. Before their marriage, my mom used to sing as she vacuumed. That was no longer allowed. If mom had the radio tuned to a Christian station, one of us would have to run to change it before he entered the house. The few times we didn't make it, you could feel the tension of his displeasure. He only had a few stations that he approved of, and none of the ones my mom liked were on his list. Also, we were running up the electric bill unnecessarily by having the radio on. My mother was told what her dress length had to be; she was not allowed to wear anything longer, even if it was in style. He even made her take a brand-new coat to be altered because it was "too long."

Their bedroom was directly across from mine. I was able to hear all of the "bedroom noises," including him tickling my mother after they were in bed. Years later, I found out that tickling is a form of abuse, and it also can be an attempt to sexually arouse another person.

Every time a repair needed to be made to the car my mother drove, a demeaning joke was made about how cars only break down when the women drive them. Belittling remarks regarding women, in general, were very common. My stepfather loved to make comments about going out with other women. Even though he knew our history, this uncaring, selfish man continued to make fictional references to the very thing that had destroyed my mother's first marriage. I could see it eroding the little bit of self-esteem she had left. He also drove the better of their two cars until the day he died.

My father had been an alcoholic for the first five years he and my mom were married before any of us were born. My mom had prayed him out of that. My stepfather knew that, but he seemed to delight in buying wine and drinking it with my mom present. The happiness they had once had was gone. My mom really tried, but when only one person is working on the marriage, it simply can't be very good.

My mother and I had brought the outside dog we'd had ever since I was very little. When she became ill with what we suspected was cancer, my stepfather refused to take her to the vet. It was too expensive, and he never had taken his dogs to the vet. So, we watched for at least a month while our precious pet went from bad to worse. She then slipped into a coma for two weeks before she died. The sounds of her dreams clearly came through my bedroom window. My agony went deep inside me as I grieved for my gentle, suffering dog.

CHAOS

All of these things did not make for a pleasant home life—again. Looking back, it is no wonder I tried to escape my miserable life by entering into "love," which I thought would be my answer.

FREE TO SOAR

STIFLE

Charm can fool you, and beauty can trick you... (Proverbs 31:30 New Century Version)

I met my handsome, brunette "knight in shining armor" at work. He seemed to be the strong, stable person I felt I desperately needed. When my boss pointed out that my good-looking co-worker wore a Christian lapel pin every day to work, that's all it took. I was hot on the trail of letting him catch me. It didn't take long. We worked together for six months before we began dating. One month after that, we were engaged. We were married three and a half months later.

Looking back, it seems so unbelievable. We thought we were waiting a long time. Erroneously, we also truly felt we knew each other. Step one just snuck up on me, and I wasn't even aware. An abuser uses his charm to coerce his way into a fast marriage, as he or she is incapable of maintaining good behavior. The charisma an abuser displays to attract a victim is not at all who he or she truly is. The genuine, voracious wolf in sheep's clothing is revealed later.

Fortunately, my father did not show up at our wedding. I was not going to have him walk me down the aisle anyway. Not long after my future groom met my unusual father, Dad had called me at work, obviously high. His words were not slurred, but collectively, they made no sense. This was another conversation in which it was his goal to make me cry, a pattern that began after he left my mother. How thoughtful of him to attempt to provoke tears in front of the people I worked with. I motioned to my future husband to pick up the other line and listen. He stayed on for a while, then quietly hung up, came to my desk, took the phone from me, and hung it up. I never heard from my father again. It has been more blissful each day that has passed without his presence in my life.

I also was grateful that my stepfather didn't come to our wedding. That was all right with me; I didn't want him there either.

We left for what we both thought was going to be a blissful honeymoon. We both had saved ourselves for this night. Yet I knew within twenty-four hours that I had made a mistake. He shut down emotionally and also showed his true colors. I discovered that what he had revealed himself to be was a false front. This is typical of abusers. They slather on the charm until they get the person they want in a situation where he or she is in the palms of their hands before they let their true character be revealed. Then the mindset is, "I did what it took to get you. Now that you're mine, I'll do whatever I want."

The way I looked at it, however, there was no turning back. I had made an oath before God, family, and friends that I would remain faithful to this man for the rest of my life. My husband knew this, too. Abusers love that undying commitment. They know you are theirs for life. They can do anything they want to, and you'll never leave them. Since I had suffered through the harrowing trauma of my parents' divorce, I was determined I would make the best of it. I was committed. Period. Nothing would ever change that—or so I thought. I was convinced and still am, that you can marry the wrong person and still have a good marriage. The clincher is that it takes two people actively working at the relationship. I worked hard at pleasing my husband, and he lived totally to please himself. That's not the right equation for a healthy relationship. The truth of the matter is that it would have been better if I had left him at that point instead of waiting until three children, a grandson, and more than twenty years had transpired.

At this time, a second step also was being played out, and I was perfectly falling prey to its ugly hands. Abusers attempt to sever their victims from all ties with family and friends. This prevents their new partners from having anywhere to run when the stages of abuse advance. If they can cut their victims off from any help in the future, then they have them right where they want them—totally under their control. The two people will then be an island totally unto themselves. Isolation is a powerful tool in the clutches of abuse. All this had begun before our marriage, yet I ignored the first signs.

Now the emotional and psychological abuse began to surface. Due to my dysfunctional upbringing, all I knew was to go along with it all. Standing up and refusing to be bullied never even entered my mind, nor had it ever been modeled in front of me at home. There had been so much dysfunction in my life that I was not even able to see that I was being disrespected. Consequently, I did not know how to assert myself and state that I was not going to be shown such disrespect. Since I didn't know either of these two things, I also did not know how to draw a boundary line and give a consequence if that happened again. I threw myself into the marriage thing, trying to ignore the negatives I was seeing. After all, one of my mother's favorite phrases she lived by was, "If you ignore something long enough, it will go away." It's too bad it took until I was almost forty years old for me to realize that her philosophy is not true. Thus, I catered to my husband's wishes. What I did not realize was that by giving in to his every whim, I was only causing his selfishness to morph into total self-absorption. Ignoring the abuse caused things to grow to the point where they eventually were out of control. I learned far too late that ignoring an abuser is enabling him or her to continue.

    Approximately two weeks after the wedding, I was pregnant, just like we had hoped for. I don't recommend this at all. Now we were adjusting to marriage, getting to know each other, dealing with the hormonal and other changes that pregnancy brings, adjusting to parenting soon, and coping with financial instability (and so much more!). Then, seven months into the pregnancy, my husband lost his job. I had quit already, so now we were in a real predicament. It was difficult not to be afraid. Although I was not aware of what the future held, being out of work would become a familiar scenario.

Our daughter was born during what turned out to be eight months of unemployment. Although my husband had begun to pull away emotionally on our honeymoon, he now pulled away even more. I found myself living with a true Tin Man. The only times he ever showed any personality were when we were around other people or when he wanted sex. He was very controlling if he didn't get what he wanted. He spent the rest of his time watching television or reading on the couch. He seemed not to care about me or our beautiful baby girl. I couldn't understand it.

I vividly recall that one day my husband turned our daughter over his knee and spanked her hard several times at the tender age of only one month because he felt she was trying to be in control. I was shaken to the core. I thought of turning him in for child abuse, but I didn't want to leave him. I still was in love with him and was optimistic about our future. We did have some good times together; they just didn't happen very often. Also, I was afraid of what he would do to make my life more miserable if I called the authorities. He had displayed enough control that I knew he was capable of more than I truly cared to imagine. I felt it was easier to ignore what I was witnessing and go on with life as I knew it than it was to rock the boat. To this day, I wonder what damage was done to our daughter both physically and emotionally, as that was not the only time he spanked her as a tiny baby.

Our daughter was five months old before he found a job. This new job required that we move—my twelfth move in twenty-one years. My life had a brief respite of peace and joy, as he enjoyed his new duties. Things went fairly well during the first three years he worked there. He was able to grow in his organizational and managerial skills and was able to work independently. He was in control, so he didn't need to control at home. That would change.

When our little girl was about a year old, we were expecting again. Just a few weeks later, we lost the baby. There had been enough emotional control exercised that I did not feel the freedom to grieve our loss. Display of emotions was not something my Tin Man husband tolerated. I stuffed my feelings down. That was a wrong choice. Less than three years later, it all came up again, like a volcano erupting. I learned a hard lesson. Now I work at freely and fully grieving whatever I am dealing with.

About six months later, I was expecting again. Then I began to recognize the all-too-familiar symptoms; I was beginning the process of losing this baby as well. I begged God to spare my child. I didn't know if I could deal with losing another little one. Then God did a miracle and spared that precious, young life. Our healthy, vigorous son was born after a full-term pregnancy. He had a strong will and was very demanding. My husband did not deal well with that at all. Through the years, this poor boy received the majority of the physical, verbal, and emotional abuse, as *no one* was to be in control of our home other than my husband. Any attempt by anyone, even a child, at displaying a strong personality was perceived by him as a threat. It never was tolerated.

The pace of my life had picked up now. I was the only one who got up with the baby at night. My husband said he needed his sleep so he could work the next day. The bed, the couch, and the kitchen table were the only places he could be found when he was at home. He would play with the children for a short time, but then the emotional door would shut, not allowing any of us in. He then became even more isolated by enveloping himself in an invisible cloak of simultaneously reading, watching TV, and listening to the radio. No one dared break through that barrier to attempt to talk to him. Yet the expectations in the bedroom were always there. It's no wonder I grew to detest his touch.

The lonely existence I had been familiar with now worsened. I was responsible for all the housework, cooking, cleaning up after meals, care of the children, laundry, and finances, as well as for a part-time job where I was on call. When he watched the children, he did not change diapers, so I couldn't be gone for very long. Yet in all my years of not being free to express myself, I did what came naturally. I let my emotions build up until I exploded. Of course, that got me nowhere, and it merely further damaged our already dying relationship.

When our son was about eighteen months old, my husband was fired from his job. This time, he only would be out of work for less than two months. Of course, his losing his job meant that we had to find somewhere else to live. We found a brand-new apartment on the second floor. Our son was absolutely fearless about running out onto our deck, often looking like he was ready to jump. Thankfully, we were always able to grab him just in time. When the ground floor unit became available six months sooner than expected, we grabbed it while we could. I broke all personal records with this move; we lived in that upstairs apartment for two weeks.

About a month after this move (number fourteen now, and I was only twenty-five), I discovered we were expecting again. This was pregnancy number four in four-and-one-half years. Gratefully, our third child, a son, slipped into the family routine very smoothly.

When our youngest son was almost a year old, we moved into our starter home. Most of the move was accomplished during the day, while my husband was at work. My routine consisted of getting up to feed the baby, waking the children to get them fed and dressed for the day, and then waking my husband while I made him a big, hot breakfast. We all then piled into the car to take him to work. After that, I picked up the girl we carpooled with and took her and our daughter to school. My sons and I would go home. Then I would pack boxes, load them into the car, put the boys back into the car, unload the boxes into the house, and then go to work at my part-time job. My daughter was brought there after school. Not long after that, I would load all three children back into the car, and we would pick my husband up from work. I remember his anger the many times I was late. Instead of standing up to him and pointing out all that was on my shoulders, I would cower. I took on his label for me that I was a bad wife who didn't have her act together.

Promptness was one way that my husband proved he was in control. He was always so very proud of himself that he was on time for everything. The whole truth was that he would give me time to be ready to leave, but he actually would be impatiently waiting ten minutes before that. I felt like such a failure. I had fallen for his psychological game and didn't even realize it. For him, being ready to leave before I was, made him feel superior to me, something he felt he desperately needed since he had such low self-esteem. Years later, as I began to get emotionally healthier, I decided to beat him at his own game. I made sure I was ready and in the car twenty minutes before we were supposed to leave to turn the tables on him. But it didn't seem to faze him at all. The only response I ever got from him was belittling, as he told me that he was proud of me, as though I were his child. I wasn't aware yet that what I was dealing with was mental abuse. At this point, feeling defeat and failure was my reaction. The few good times we used to have were now infrequent. I began to feel so alone.

STIFLE

By this time, emotional withdrawal, arrogance, and control were my husband's trademarks. I approached an older man that I knew my husband respected in an attempt to get help in dealing with our life at home. He brought another gentleman along, and together, they confronted my husband about things they had seen. I was relieved that they cared enough to talk to him, but in the end, it made no difference at all.

When our youngest son was just a few months old, we were given a lively puppy. He was a delight, but also a lot of work. I wonder if you can guess who essentially took care of him. That's right. I fed him and cleaned up after him. Only in very rare instances did I put my foot down and insist that my husband clean up the mess. It's amazing for me to see, now that I look back on it, that when I did stand up for myself or the children, he would back down. That's unheard of with abusers and dangerous for his victims.

The only time my husband helped to care for the dog was when he took him outside, but he did it without a leash. He did not agree with the leash law; therefore, he didn't abide by it. The dog was not obedience trained, and he came back to the house when he felt like it. I lashed out at my husband the day the dog got hit by a car. He tried to tell me what to do to help him get the dog to the vet. But I put my foot down and told him I wasn't going to do a thing; this was his fault for not using a leash. I felt horrible for the dog but knew I had to stand my ground. My husband knew I was right. The dog would have been fine if he'd been properly cared for by being on a leash. My husband backed down and didn't argue with me. After the dog came back from the veterinarian's, my husband used a leash on him for a long time. He never once uttered a word about it, but by his actions, he showed that he knew he had been wrong.

Feeling helpless and hopeless, I let it all slide into a mundane, daily existence. Since I had four people to feed, clean up after, and keep in fresh clothes, it was anything but mundane. Our home did not have the true tone of love in it. My busyness helped me to ignore what actually was going on. Fortunately, I did not allow it to stay that way forever.

CONFUSION

I know that You, God, are on the side of victims... (Psalms 140:12 MSG)

Life became a tiresome rut, and I seemed to fall asleep to the reality around me. It was easy to miss the changes that came. My husband was the one who brought the changes, but they were so subtle that they essentially went unnoticed. Abusers are masters at this. Their approach is like a cat stealthily moving toward its prey. The movements are detectable to an alert observer, but the intended victim ordinarily is oblivious to it all. My husband was no exception. He never could have had as much power early in our marriage, when I was more alert, as he did right before I left him. No, for him the obsession with total control was something to be schemed, with timing and cunning being twin, key ingredients for his success.

Church was the essence of our life as a family, as it was the only place we were allowed to socialize. Silently and subtly, it was made clear that we were not to get too close to anyone and certainly not to open up to them.

Attending church essentially revolved around my husband, as it gave him a chance to play his role as the perfect family man who had it all together. The image had been all too important to him for many years. He pushed himself into a lower-end leadership level, just as he had at the first church we attended together. He loved his titles, both there and at his new job. I think it also was satisfying to him since he had been told growing up that he never would amount to anything. It seemed to give him a sense of importance and authority. In the years to follow, this grew completely out of hand. He became a totally different person than I ever had known. After about ten years of marriage, I began to wake up to reality. I was in a marriage with an emotionally detached man who abused all of us as he lived his own life that was centered around his favorite person: himself. I felt caught, trapped. The rare good times that we used to have pretty much had stopped. Hopelessness set in. I saw no way out. And I knew he would get worse than ugly if I went to such drastic measures as leaving. Also, since the children were still little, there would be custody issues, along with quite a bit of contact with him over things like transporting them and dealing with school matters.

What I saw as an answer was a complete break from him. Because I was afraid of my own husband, I would not want him to know where the children and I lived. We would leave, he never would have a clue where we were, and we never would have to speak to him again. But I knew that the whole scenario never would work. He had strong ties with three law enforcement agencies, and he would utilize every one of them to locate us. I had seen him use those methods to find other people. He would pull out all the stops to find the children and me. He then would use his power, control, and twisted words to get us to come back to him.

There also was a financial issue. I could not stand the thought of having to work fulltime to support the kids and myself. I had believed the lie he had told me that I could never survive if I had to work outside the home. I also did not see how I ever could find a job that would pay enough to support the four of us. It was hard enough to make ends meet. I could not imagine having to deal with abject poverty alone. I didn't think I could find child care that I could trust in a completely new town. I had observed my mother's agony before, during, and after my parents were divorced, and I did not think I had the emotional strength to endure that kind of anguish. I was beaten down as it was. I didn't think I could handle things being any worse.

Then there was the mere thought of our three precious children, whom I loved with all my heart, being torn in two between their parents, feeling they had to side with one or the other. I still could feel the intense pain of it all from my childhood. There was no way I wanted to expose my children to that deep sorrow.

During this time, my husband expanded his sexual abuse to more than just me. This went on for years. One of his victims attempted to bring it to light at the time the sexual abuse was going on, but my husband was able to do his usual verbal tap dance and get out of it smelling like a rose. Years later, it was confirmed when one of the victims began to open up to the other. The details were too horrifically identical. I believe beyond a shadow of a doubt that the abuse did take place. My husband should have been thrown in prison, but

CONFUSION

the statute of limitations had run out by the time all of this came to light.

Ironically, during the time all this was going on, we were doing prison ministry. That's right. The very place we went each week was where he belonged. I shudder each time I think about what went on without my knowing about it. Now we all suffer from the pain of what happened. I have agonized over it, but there is no way to go back in time and live it differently. I have had to leave it in God's capable hands. I don't want to waste my time with what I'm not able to go back and repair. When I have lived in regret, it has drained my energy. I have too much purpose in my life now to wallow in the past. (I will add here that I don't think it would be possible for me to cope with all that I have been through if I didn't know that my Father is the Vindicator for my children and me. God saw to it that this truth was firmly planted within me shortly after I left my husband.)

It is interesting to note that I had made it clear from the beginning of our marriage and on numerous occasions that I would leave immediately if I ever found out that my husband was unfaithful to me. Also, each time I saw on the news that someone had been accused or convicted of any sexual impropriety with a child, I told him in no uncertain terms that I never would tolerate that. As I look back now, his facial response was a dead giveaway. The unspoken, arrogant reply given with a twinkle in his eye and a slightly evil smirk stated that he was getting away with it now and would continue to because he knew he wouldn't be caught anyway.

In my mind, if I ignored this long enough, it would all go away. (Remember my mother's philosophy?) Denial was my coping mechanism. Because of that, I didn't look into it any further. If I had, that would have meant facing the reality of it all. To do that would have meant an even harder row to hoe than I already had. I was too bogged down with the weight of everything. Not only would I not have known where to begin, but also it would have meant even more intense pain for all of us, a court case, jail time, plus our two families and the entire community knowing. It just seemed to be more than I was able to endure. The right thing to do is not always easy. I chose the easier way, but it wasn't necessarily right.

CONFUSION

One very positive thing I found out after I left my husband was that following several years of sexual abuse, one of his victims confronted him. That child told him that it was known that what he had been doing was wrong and that his actions had a name: sexual abuse. The child told my husband that if he ever tried it again, the authorities would be called. He never touched that child again.

In the last several years before I left, my husband had become very demanding, coercive, emotionally forceful, and controlling in order to have sex. Later, as I found out about the sexual abuse, it all fit together like a puzzle that had missing pieces. His behavior changed because his victim had stood up to him and he no longer had that additional outlet.

I have every reason to believe that my husband had a sexual addiction, just as my father had, as well as being a pedophile. One thing I never could get away from was what he expected from me in the bedroom. For me, it ceased to be something pleasurable. My enjoyment wasn't even considered. And if he did bring it up, it was still with a twist so that it was his pleasure that was the bottom line and I was made out to be the one with a problem. He was such a master at these types of conversations that it was nearly impossible to unravel it all to get down to the truth, no matter what the subject matter was. Even when what I wanted was discussed, he didn't listen, because the bottom line was still the bottom line: him. Even when we'd had tension between us and it was still unresolved, I was expected to be responsive in the bedroom within forty-eight hours.

Unemployment soon reared its ugly head again. We now had a mortgage, a car payment, and three children and a dog to care for, but we had no income. Somehow during that time, if my husband wanted to play ball on a team, the money always was there to pay his part of the entry fee. Yet we were only able to afford for our children to take swimming lessons one summer in all their years at home. Also, our growing children were all wearing underwear that was too small and mine was full of holes, my husband saw the need to have sports glasses, to the tune of $75 that we didn't have. Again, the money appeared somehow. Eventually, our sons were able to play ball for

CONFUSION

more than one season, but our daughter never got to do the things that would have benefited her physically. Financial abuse and neglect had struck again, yet I was blind as a bat. Emotionally, I felt beaten down and helpless.

More than once, we were the family that was adopted for Christmas. What a blessing, but also, how humiliating. It was overwhelming to see the love that was poured out on us by complete strangers.

When unemployment ran out, we had no choice but to apply for welfare. I didn't know how much lower we could go. Yet my husband refused to be the one to apply. He said he just couldn't face going into the office. That left only one person: me. It was devastating. Even though he was out of work, he wouldn't even watch our children while I went in to file the paperwork. To this day, I don't understand why. I do know that he was self-absorbed and staying at home with the children was a duty he clearly didn't want. Yet in this instance, was it laziness, feeling guilty, or feeling inadequate as a provider? Whatever the reason, I asked my mom to accompany me to the welfare office to help me with the children. How much more oppressed could I possibly feel?

I remember that depressing, heavy visit vividly. Looking back, I should have refused to go. Maybe then he would have either applied for welfare or gone out to find even a low-paying job. Since I did what he should have done, I was enforcing the fact that I would rescue him, and also that I would continue to allow him to manipulate me.

Finally, after two very long years of being unemployed, my husband found a job. From the beginning, he was required to be a jerk as a part of this new profession. How delightful! The controller he had been at home now morphed into a monster.

This new occupation only required that he be in the office half the day. The remainder of his time was to be spent on the road. He used this new freedom to pop in on us unexpectedly throughout the day. He said it was because he wanted to see us, but it began to feel as though it was to keep tabs on us. Because he was behind the wheel for so many hours, he began to follow us when the children and I had to run errands. I'll never forget the first evening he

CONFUSION

came home and told us all the places where we had been that day. He was so proud of himself. I don't believe I ever saw such a big smile on his face. He looked like the proud cat that had swallowed the canary. An eerie fear poured over me. I suddenly felt as though I could not make a single move without him knowing about it. If I had been miserable before with what it was like for all of us to live with him, I was heavily laden now. It was as though I had no hope of ever escaping his ever-watchful eye. Now I felt my every move was being kept under surveillance twenty-four hours a day. I empathized with a hunted animal and wondered if I ever could feel free again.

To make things worse, this stalking scenario was repeated numerous times. I never knew when I left home if he was watching or not. One thing that made it easier for him was that he always made sure we had a one-of-a-kind vehicle. I rarely saw him in my rearview mirror as we drove around town. He became stealthy with this new game of his. The children even began to watch for him. It upset them, but I don't recall that they ever said anything to him about it. He loved following us and then proudly talking about it when he arrived home. Each time this was repeated, it seemed to put additional weight on my shoulders. The control became more and more suffocating.

I was in such inner turmoil. No matter what angle I approached all of this from, the only conclusion I could come up with was to stay. Surely, I thought, it would be better for us to remain under the same roof with him. Hindsight seems to prove to be a 20/20 vision. I know now that many organizations are waiting out there to assist victims and their helpless children as they begin new lives. Not only was I not aware of that then, but also many of them weren't in existence at that time. Even counseling is now available either at no or low cost to assist everyone in the family through the difficult transition time. I never cease to be amazed at all the resources that are offered.

The bottom line is that I should have pulled us all out. Although it would have been tough, I firmly believe the kids and I would have been fine in the end. I often think of how different each of them would be now if I had. But I cannot live my life in regret. I've asked my children and Jesus, to forgive me. I have put

CONFUSION

the past in God's hands. My focus has got to be on both the present and the future.

So instead of leaving, I plowed on the best that I could. By now, we all were experiencing abuse from this man—emotional, verbal, and financial. The children were physically abused as well, but he knew never to touch me. I had drawn that line in the sand early in our marriage, and he knew never to cross that. Looking back, it seems odd that I wouldn't allow him to hurt me physically when the pain he inflicted was much worse than any bruise or cut would have been.

My inner turbulence had reached a point where I felt like I was living in an emotional tornado. And I, too, began to physically abuse our children. My husband had convinced me this was the way to discipline them. Since it was all I ever had known, I had no real argument to present. Again, I found it easier to follow the path that had been shown to me by the strong, intimidating leader in our home.

Many years later, when I read the book *The Whisper* by Shirley Jo Petersen, I found several things to be so very helpful. This quote is one example from her book that explained my behavior: "What the children said and wanted quickly triggered the compliance channel in my mind to do as I was told. Consequently, Jim (husband) became involved in much of the disciplining at home. I remember him asking me, '...why are you letting them do that? Remember, you're the adult here, the one in charge.' Jim's suggestions not only made me aware of my problem but also facilitated the needed changes in me. I found myself repeating Jim's words, 'Remember, I'm the adult here, so I need to take charge and do what is right.' New thought patterns and habits take time."[4] Because I had complied with my surroundings all my life, I honestly didn't know what it was like to be in charge. It's at times like this that I see so clearly how dysfunction hurts. Yet again, I cannot live in regret. I did that for too long and experienced the damage that does. I've got to move forward and pray that my children can do so as well.

    At one point, we had a friend who sat us down and began to confront my husband. She had been coming to a Bible study he taught in our home. She clearly spelled out the problems

CONFUSION

she had with him in a very loving and respectful way. This was a wonderful wake-up call, as I saw that she was 100% correct in everything she told him. I was terrified, waiting for her to turn to me next.

I finally saw a chance in their interchange to ask about problems she had with me. She had none. I was speechless. It was one step in seeing that maybe our secret problems weren't entirely my fault as he always had said. Just maybe I wasn't the awful person he tried to convince me that I was.

I began to push for counseling for my husband and me. I knew we were badly in need of help. I felt desperate for guidance. I couldn't even think for myself anymore. Every idea had to be passed through my husband. I don't believe I had original thought processes functioning at this point. My thinking had been muddied by his opinions. However, my husband saw no need to go to see anyone. From the very first, I had heard nothing but harsh, negative remarks about all those in the field of mental health. So I took an approach that I hoped would be a little more tolerated. I called our church. After several months of counseling there, we gained absolutely no ground.

I soon was referred elsewhere. Gladly, I saw a woman who helped me work through all sorts of issues, even those dating back to my childhood that had gone unresolved. This delightful woman helped me deal with my anger problem. Our children began coming to me and saying that I had changed. It felt so good to be getting rid of the emotional trash pile that had accumulated inside of me. At the end of the year, my counselor said she was amazed at the progress I had made. That meant so much to hear her say that, as my self-esteem was nonexistent at that time.

We could only afford for one of us to go see a counselor at any one time. So after about a year of me seeing my counselor, my husband began to go by himself. Knowing it would be a better fit, he saw a male therapist. He pulled his usual verbal stunts of blaming me. He had in every session we had been in together, and that wasn't about to change. Yet he did it in such a crafty, smooth way that even the professionals didn't catch him. To date, I haven't seen anyone as shrewd as he is, except for his brother. It was

CONFUSION

extremely rare when my husband admitted fault in anything. It is no wonder I was so confused. I have heard similar stories repeated by other men and women who have left their abusers.

We were soon referred to a woman who specialized in working with children. She did a lot of work with us as a family. However, there wasn't much progress made when this single lady tried to do marriage counseling. One positive thing that came from those sessions was that she was able to get my husband to admit he had been jealous of our children from day one. I had suspected that and even asked him more than once. Yet he never would admit to it. I now understood his seeming disinterest in them. How sad to be so immature or emotionally ill that you neglect your responsibility to parent your own children.

I was beyond weary of trying to make excuses for him to my family. I usually would say that due to a lack of funds we were unable to contribute to family dinners; yet he would have the latest in sports glasses to wear. (Keep in mind that our children never had an eye exam until they left home, as we couldn't afford it. I had bad eyesight and would wait until the headaches drove me to the eye doctor. Even then, it was a financial juggling act to get that paid for.)

My husband would not come to some of my family gatherings, yet they knew he was not sick. There was no way I was going to tell them the truth that he did not want to be around any of them because he didn't like them. I didn't want to rock the boat with him or with the family, but I should have. In contrast, when it came time for his family to get together, he *always* went. My family knew this as well. Covering up for his actions had gone beyond ridiculous and to the point that it angered me. I felt rejected, hurt, confused, anxious, and depressed regarding our marriage. Since he blamed me for our problems, I partially blamed myself, too. I also was afraid to make him upset in any way. I wasn't sure just how badly he would react, and I certainly didn't want to find out. Although I didn't see it at the time, this was the same pattern I'd learned with my father.

This emotional and psychological abuse was no picnic. Not only did he continue to tell me that I never would be able to make it on my own, but he also constantly belittled all of us.

CONFUSION

No one could come up with a solution as grand as his perfect ideas. Frequently, he either ignored my thoughts or grandly presented his own. Then as time went on, he would have a brilliant inspiration—the very answer I had given in the beginning. He merely wanted me to believe that he was in control and that I was totally in need of him. It kept me afraid of my ability to succeed without his wisdom to guide me. This also added to my confusion.

The children received more verbal abuse than I did. Since he had been told all through his childhood that he never would amount to anything, he, thankfully, didn't say those things directly to our children or me. However, his conversations with all of us were heavily laden with those unspoken, demeaning words. You see, if he could control our thinking, he could control us. If he could control us, then he was still in control of everything that took place in our home. It was as though we all lived in his little moat-protected castle.

My husband seemed to despise our children's attempts at learning to think for themselves. Yet he was constantly after them, especially during their preteen and teenage years, to think on their own. When they did, he would object because it wasn't his decision that had been made. They would defend their choices, saying that they had done what he always had told them to do: think for themselves. When they reminded him of this, one of his favorite retorts to them was, "Well, don't." The tone of it all was that they had made a stupid choice and were incapable of making a good decision. Once they were in their late teens, they could see through him. The bottom line was that any of us could make the decision that he would have made, but if *he* wasn't the one who thought of it, then the decision was the wrong one. This put him at the center of the universe. He was the only one who was right.

This narcissism is extremely difficult to live with. Those who live under the same roof with anyone like this do so in an almost constant state of frustration and get beaten down emotionally and mentally, as you simply can't win. The confusion that is produced is never-ending. The only way to find the road out is to have someone who can see above the walls of this foggy, dark maze guide you to the exit. The good counselors I have been privileged to see have done exactly that. Insanity has been defined as doing the same thing over and over again, yet expecting different results. I never would have gotten out of the confusing swirl of my husband's abuse if I'd never had help. I'm forever grateful.

More financial abuse followed closely behind verbal abuse. It seemed the manipulation and control had to be established before he could be in control of the money. I had been pretty good at handling finances before this, but his logic was that he was in the right. He reasoned that when we got married, he had more cash saved up from his previous job than I had. The point that he had been paid a much higher hourly wage conveniently never entered the picture. He was always right. Even if he wasn't, he could twist the conversation around until he sounded as though he was. I'm grateful he was never on the debate team in school. It was difficult enough to live with his arguments. It would have been worse if he'd mastered this skill beyond his natural ability.

Two times my husband bought a classic or antique car to be used as the only car for our family. At all times, they were to be in pristine condition, perfectly clean, and ready to be put in a car show. He used the excuse that they were the best cars out there in our price range. However, because of their age, the needed repairs became a real drain on our finances. But if something went wrong with one of them, money seemingly would be pulled out of the hat to repair them. One year, he used our tax refund to pay for a new paint job so that the vehicle could be put in car shows. Yet the children and I went without needed items. That in a nutshell is both neglect and financial abuse. The house also needed improvements, and our savings was nonexistent. It didn't matter. His desires were met, and he owned the car he wanted; he was the priority.

At this point, we still were recovering from his third round of unemployment. For those who never have been through this, it can take a long time to bounce back from that financial hardship. For me, it seemed that I needed to scrutinize each purchase closely, as I never knew when they would come to the attention of my husband's hawk eye. If an expense didn't center on him, then the money was spent incorrectly. If I didn't get the groceries he was wanting, then I hadn't bought the right things. Even though he didn't tell me what he was craving before I went, I was still in the wrong for not buying it. If I had purchased essentials and there was no money for something fun like he wanted, I was still in the wrong because I hadn't done as good of a job as I could have. Shopping was never something I enjoyed doing, but it had become something I feared. To this day, I still fight a certain dread of having to shop for essentials. There are times that I find myself short of breath and slightly panicky while in a store, wondering if my money will stretch or if I'm purchasing something that I don't need.

Until the day I left him, my husband begrudgingly allowed family funds to be spent on the children if they were outgrowing their clothes. His preference was to have it spent on his interests. It never ceased to amaze me how money always was there to repair his car, replace the ball glove he repeatedly lost, or buy new clothes for him. Yet when there was a real need for the children or myself, he would just shrug it off and say he wished he could help but there was nothing he could do.

FREE TO SOAR

To give a couple of examples, at one point I had to make twenty dollars stretch to feed the five of us for a week. This went on for months. Also, my sewing skills came in handy as I taught myself how to patch holes in my underwear and sometimes in the children's, as the money simply wasn't there to buy new ones. I got to the point where I almost could account for every penny spent. Then after all that hard work, my husband would blow money on totally foolish and unnecessary things when he felt like it. One time, our church gave us money for our rent. He bought a microwave instead. I should have turned him into them for mismanaging their generous gift, but I was too afraid of what I would have to live with afterward. Another time, he bought a VCR at a garage sale because he saw we had the money in the checking account. We did, but it was sitting there to cover a utility bill that hadn't come in the mail yet.

The straw that broke the camel's back was when he came and asked if we had ten dollars. I looked in the check register and told him we didn't. He went out anyway and bought a complete set of baseball cards for ten dollars.

CONFUSION

His logic was that they were half-price and an investment for the future. This was not the first time he'd done this type of thing; this was his pattern. The last few times, I had threatened to turn all of the finances over to him if he did it again. I don't think he ever took me seriously. This time, I was furious. I went and got the checkbook and slapped it against his chest. He couldn't believe I was doing that. I told him if he was going to spend like this, then he could have the entire responsibility for the money. I told him that from now on he was going to pay all the bills, balance the checkbook, and I was not going to help him at all. I was scared, but I'd had more than I could tolerate. I should have done it sooner. Again, I want to point out that when I stood up to him, he backed down. I recall how peacefully I slept that night, knowing the responsibility of our money matters was now off my sagging shoulders. The part I found humorous was that he said he hardly slept at all, as he had taken a good look at the checkbook and our bills and seen the reality of where our funds were. In the years that followed, his pattern of purchasing what he wanted when he wanted it still went on, but with less frequency.

For years, I gave haircuts to our boys to save money. Once I got pretty good, I wanted him to let me cut his to save even more on our tight budget. Yet my husband continued to pay for his until he felt my self-taught skill passed his inspection. Years later, I regretted those pleas of mine, as it meant I had to stand close to him for a long time. The closer I had to be to him, the more I could feel the awful spirits he was operating under; being near him made me squirm.

When he took a new job out of town, it was obvious I would need a used vehicle for around town. He found a used one, and the insurance was reasonable. However, it was so interesting to see the pattern that emerged. If my car needed repairs, I would have to wait. Yet if his needed something minor, it was fixed right away. For example, for more than an entire summer, I had to drive my van around town without air conditioning in it. He was in no hurry to fix it. Yet during this time, he had minor repairs done on his vehicle. Then my driver's window stopped working, which left

CONFUSION

only one window for air circulation in a full-size van. I firmly told him that in the spring it *would* be repaired, as I refused to drive a preheated oven for another summer. Within a couple of weeks, it was taken care of. Since it was so rare that I spoke up and insisted on anything, I didn't see the pattern of how he backed down when I became assertive. How different would our lives have been if I had gone toe-to-toe with him more often? That's a question that I probably never will have answered. It would also have been very risky.

One thing I never dared to do was take his pay stubs, add all the bills and the money he gave me for groceries and then see what was left over for him to spend as he desired. I was terrified that I would see a large amount of money unaccounted for and lose control of myself and yell at him to find out what he was doing with it all. I had pinched pennies for so long that I was beginning to feel like a nervous wreck. I have a hunch he was taking a sizable amount from each paycheck, but I'll never know. By this point in time, he was making fairly good money, especially for what we had been accustomed to. Yet the money allotted for groceries hadn't gone up.

The interesting thing is that one of my husband's pet peeves that he taught against was blame-shifting. Yet he loved to pin the fault onto someone else rather than take responsibility for wrong behavior. I believe he hated what he was, but either he didn't know how to change, didn't want to, or was horrified at the thought of having his image changed with us and before others. I don't believe he wanted to change, as that would have meant the future was unpredictable, which meant it would be out of his control. Control was the only way he ever had been able to feel secure. I believe the thought of losing that was terrifying to him. He didn't know any other way to relate to anyone around him.

Finally, I'd had more than I could take. I got in touch with a friend who had called me on the false front we were leading. She had seen through it all. While I poured out my pain in halting sentences, she patiently and lovingly listened. Through her help and others, we contacted that day, we confronted him. I asked for a short separation. It was terrifying. I never would have had the backbone to do that on my own. I knew it could completely backfire on me, as I knew it would stir up his anger. But I could not continue to live like that; nor could I continue to see our children brought up in that craziness. The years of counseling we had gone through had not helped our marriage at all. The few good times we'd had together were now only a memory. I had not seen any changes in him, even when he had seen a counselor for almost a year. I was at my wits' end at this point, and I knew our lives could not possibly go on as they had been.

After two agonizing weeks, I asked him to come back. Looking back on it now, it seems unthinkable. That should have been the end of our insidious life. However, I allowed several things to be woven together as the basis for my choice, including the fear of the future, an "inability" to financially care for myself and the children, my "incapability" to hold down a fulltime job, memories of my mother's agony after my parent's divorce and her constant fatigue due to working over forty hours a week to provide for us, the torment that my husband would put me through regarding visitation with the children if I filed for divorce, how he would try to turn the children against me, the emotional turmoil the children would go through, and all the other legal muck I would be drug through.

The separation only caused this emotional tornado within me to swirl faster and faster. I knew him well enough to know that he would stalk and constantly harass us. His control simply would worsen. He would do all that he could to make our lives miserable. It would be like a game to him, much as a cat plays with a mouse before eliminating it. This would be a new, unending lifestyle for our children and me. I was worn out and felt unable to deal with it by myself. No matter how I looked at it, still, it seemed a better choice to remain under the same roof with him. It seemed that what we were now enduring was not as bad as what we would have experienced if we had left.

Looking back, I know that I just should have had each of us throw a sheet on the floor and put on them the things we would need, our legal documents, and our most prized possessions.

CONFUSION

Then we should have wrapped each sheet up and left. But I didn't know where I would go. Since then, I've seen that I would not have been alone at all. As I've stated before, some individuals and organizations would have collectively seen me through it all. It's never impossible to leave an abuser. The National Domestic Violence Hotline, 1-800-799-SAFE (7233), is a good first step. Don't ever think any situation is impossible. There is *always* a way out. The people waiting to help the victims are more than capable of helping to keep them safe, supporting them through the legal battles, and assisting them in starting their lives over. That's what they specialize in.

It wasn't long before what I term "spiritual abuse" began to come into play. We were not allowed to have a belief different from my husband's. The pattern of this was still hidden from me, as I was still the frog slowly being boiled to death in the water, not knowing I simply could jump out.

Due to distance and other factors, we soon needed to find a church closer to where we lived. Once we found the one we both were comfortable with, it didn't take my husband long to wheedle his way into the leadership of this undiscerning group of people. I had agreed to his idea of having a new beginning now that we were back together again and not telling anyone of our two-week separation. So now the image we presented had to be perfect. He worshipped at the feet of his goodness. It was disgusting, and our children were seeing his façade now. About a year before I left him, he became a deacon. Our teenage children and I vehemently opposed him on this. Then an ugly situation arose within the church. He had said he would do one thing, yet when faced with the decision in front of all the people he had tried to impress, he backed down and sided with the rest of the leaders. Clearly, his image was of the highest importance—more important than what was right. As I sat there during those proceedings, with him on the other side of the room with the rest of the leaders he had declared he would not sit by, one part of me longed to have him at my side. The other part of me felt it was normal to have him totally separated—both physically and theologically. He already had created this chasm between us years before, during our honeymoon. This simply seemed to seal it. There was a finality of sorts during that meeting, a true severing of our marriage. I lost any respect I had left for him.

I hesitate in bringing this up, as I don't want anyone immediately to begin looking with suspicion at every pastor or leader in a church as a possible abuser or another type of hypocrite. Some fantastic people are serving in these capacities that are living the life of genuine Christians. This simply is another unfortunate piece of my story.

Less than two years after our separation, we moved into a larger house. We had been terribly cramped in our starter home. I will admit it had been nice for me to live in the same house for twelve years, but we had needed a change for a very long time. It was so nice for each of us finally to have our own private space to retreat to. The main reason for the move was the hope that it would alleviate some of the tension in our marriage. As I look back now, it's obvious to me that new surroundings were not the answer. It's impossible to resurrect something dead simply by moving it from one building to another.

FREE TO SOAR

TWISTED

Call on Me when you are in trouble and I will rescue you... (Psalm 50:15a NLT)

I finally began to get some help in the last few years of our marriage. As I started to untangle all the twistedness of my husband's philosophies, I began to confront him with the truth of what I saw. And as our children came to me with their frustrations about their father, I did my best to help them unravel the garbage he had dealt them. They were very observant and already could see what he truly was; there was no way to hide that from them. I believe that being able to get the truth out into the open helped them to deal with things better. I saw it as a situation similar to that of a neighborhood bully. If a child understands the bully, the child will be able to deal with that difficult person in a much healthier way. This was not without its own struggles, though, as I knew what I told them would only cause them to disrespect him even more. My only other option was total to support him. My perceptive children would be able to see through that, though, and I would lose their trust. It was a flimsy tightrope I walked. I opted for honesty in the hopes of as much emotional health for them as possible. Time would reveal if I was right or not.

The kids soon began to confront him, both individually and by arranging it ahead of time so that they all were there together. This is when I began to see a true change in him. He knew he was losing control of us. He now began to morph into someone I never had seen before, and it was scary. He tried more coercion, more oppressive rules, and stronger manipulation to intimidate us. It didn't work. The more he pushed us, the more confident we became. With all four of us in agreement, we felt empowered. I don't know how our children felt, but I know I was scared. Yet we continued telling him what was true—not what he wanted to hear.

All of his actions revealed that he was boiling mad over all this. I believe that if there ever was a time he wanted to physically abuse me, it was then. Yet he was a man who prided himself on being in control. He never wanted it said that he had lost restraint, even though I had seen that happen twice when he kicked our little dog down the basement steps. He came close a few other times, but he pulled himself together with that classic control of his. Also, he remembered that I had drawn a line in the sand early in our marriage; I told him that if he ever hit me, I would leave. His response had been a chilling reply, dripping with forcefulness and manipulation, "...and if you leave, you'll never be allowed to come back." That instilled such terror in me. I look back now and realize that was due to the evil spirit that was behind it all. He had physically abused the children and our precious dog, but he never physically abused me. It still amazes me that he never crossed that line. Was it because I drew that boundary? I doubt that I'll ever know the answer to that.

There is one evening that will be emblazoned in my memory forever. It was to be our date night. (Oh, how I grew to hate that weekly occurrence!) The plans were that we would be staying home to talk. Both of our sons were going out for the evening. After the first son left the house, my husband locked the back screen door. As the next son left through the front door, my husband got up from the couch where we were both seated, followed our son to the door, and proceeded to lock that screen door as well. His unspoken message was crystal clear to me. No one would be able to enter the house to help me while he carried out whatever he had in mind.

As he turned back around, his eyes were like nothing I ever had seen before from him. There was a demonic look in his eyes as he looked directly at me. Chills and terror ran through my body. I truly wondered if I would survive the night. It was a turning point for him. All I recall about that evening is that he verbally laid into me. Of course, woven into the words was the typical twisted emotional abuse he had mastered so well. Now, this was coupled with the other-worldly power he had tapped into. I'll probably never know if he had more than that "talk" planned, but I was relieved to find myself still alive hours later when it was time for bed. How I ever laid my head on the pillow and went to sleep that night with him next to me is more than I can comprehend.

One physical problem I still have today is a tense left shoulder from sleeping with my husband on my left side. If my arm touched him, especially before we fell asleep, it would "inspire" him. I felt so used, so filthy. The last few months before I left him, when he was finished having his fun, I immediately would get out of bed, get dressed, and leave the room for as long as I dared. If I stayed gone too long, though, he eventually would come out to find me. I then would be scolded in that horrid, controlling, terrifying way that he had. Essentially, I was told that I needed to come back to bed, as a wife should always sleep with her husband, and he couldn't fall asleep without me there.

    I remember one of those nights. I came out of our bedroom and ran into our younger son. He kept asking me what was wrong. I'm sure he never had seen that look on my face before. I truly couldn't answer him. I was beyond angry. I felt so absolutely slimed. I muttered something in reply to him, but I couldn't confide in my sixteen-year-old son. I left it at saying that my fury was directed at his father. This put further guilt on me for turning his heart even more against his own dad. Yet he lovingly wouldn't let me go without an explanation of some kind. Both of my sons were so caring and protective of me. I know if they'd had any idea of what went on when they weren't around, the insidiousness would have stopped long before it did.

During the rare times when we were able to go out for the evening, I dreaded it, as I knew what was expected in the bedroom as repayment for a meal out. If I accompanied him on a business trip out of town, I knew what was expected in the hotel room. As we drove, he controlled what we listened to, even if I brought along music I thought we both would enjoy. Traveling with him was miserable. He was such a controller; he could not relax his hold on anything—he had to be in charge of it all. He would ask me where I wanted to stop and eat. It wouldn't matter, though. We ate where he wanted to. For him to ask me became an additional weight on me emotionally, as my opinion didn't matter anyway. It was just another emotional game for him to play against me.

There was no spark of originality in our home. Fun was squelched before it truly began. I lived for the time he would leave for work. Yet even then, I was so beaten down that I had to work hard at having an original thought geared toward relaxation with the kids. When he left the house, a great weight of oppression left with him. Yet we all were victims of his abuse and control, so we really couldn't enjoy each other. We were all so highly dysfunctional. He controlled where we went, what we did, what we thought, who we spoke to, and who we avoided. Our teenagers didn't matter. I didn't matter. Our opinions were unimportant. He was center stage, and no one else was even in the cast of his stage presentation.

My personal possessions were not shown respect by him. One Sunday I handed him some treasured maracas a friend had brought back for me from her trip to Mexico. Instead of putting them someplace safe in the car, he put them on the floor of the back seat. Our son stepped on them and broke them. My husband couldn't have cared less; our son couldn't apologize enough. Yet when it was a possession of my husband's, we all had to treat it with extra care. This imbalance clearly shows me where I stood with him; yet I couldn't see this at the time. As I look back, it is a clear indication of his total lack of respect for me as his wife. I believe now that he put those maracas on the floorboard on purpose. For example, I knew his car ranked way above me. So did the dog. How secure can you feel when the car and dog are loved and you are used?

I felt so trapped in my marriage. At our wedding, I had pledged my life to him, and I meant it. I had seen firsthand the extreme pain that comes from divorce. I'd promised before God and those who attended our wedding that I was going to stay with him until death. I meant it. But now I not only felt stuck but also very scared as to what my future with him would look like. Without his saying a thing, I could sense his desire to get his revenge on me by hurting me physically. He had proven to me many, many times through the years that he was stronger than I was. He always made sure that was very clear. I felt terror, total defeat, and hopelessness as a constant weight over my head.

It got to the place where I honestly can say that I don't remember receiving any respect from him, even as a fellow human being. When I would come home from the store with supplies and groceries for two weeks, he would stay in the living room while I unloaded it all from the car, brought it inside, and put it away.

For several years, I did have one friend I could talk to, but she was in a similar situation. We were only comparing notes as we vented. She had no solutions either. I began to feel desperate. I couldn't talk to anybody, as it would compromise my husband's position both at work and church. I knew his main fear was having his image tarnished. My eldest son told me about the mothers of two of his friends. He said I should get to know them, that we really would get along. I was more than hesitant. My self-esteem had been smashed to bits. I finally did get to know them. It took a few years, but I eventually dared to open up with each of them. Their concern, support, and offers to help let me know that we were definitely in a bad situation. I realized that maybe I wasn't crazy after all, that possibly it was my circumstances that were certifiably off the wall and not me.

Let me stop here and say that if someone is opening up to you about a relationship he or she is in, please listen. That person actually may be reaching out for help. Ask questions. You're not prying. If there is any kind of abuse going on, the person is only telling you the mild things. Then if that person feels he or she can trust you, he or she will open up even more. Lovingly ask questions. Find out more about the story. What has shocked me more than anything is the common response I've heard from dear friends who I thought knew what was going on. The shared remark after reading the manuscript for this book is that they had no idea this was going on. One man, who is like a brother to me, told his wife that if he had known what life was like for us, he would have given me the money to get away. Another man said if he had known he would have seen to it that the children and I got out safely. Your inquiries won't be snooping into the other person's personal life; they will be from a heart of love. No one should have to live through what my children and I experienced. *Your questions may save at least one life.*

About twenty years into my dysfunctional marriage, I began to get together with a few friends regularly. I knew I could trust these women completely. We discussed our tough issues at home. The time spent with these women became such a source of strength for me. We became more vulnerable with one another and shared advice. It wasn't always easy to hear the truth, but it brought us out of denial into reality and gave us coping mechanisms. These were deep, deep conversations. There was an intangible wealth that came from months of this. I finally was getting the help I needed.

As a result, I began to get healthier emotionally. The healthier I became, the more I confronted my husband. The more I stood up to him and told him the truth, the angrier he became. Yet I would go through this intense cycle again if it were necessary to get to where I am today. Of course, his anger was controlled. On the outside, he said less. Yet our children and I noticed that the atmosphere around him was changing. The air was thick with tension any time he was home. When he pulled out of the driveway for work each morning, it felt as though even the house sighed with relief. Each day, about an hour, before he was due home, fear and dread seemed to smother the oxygen out of my lungs and prevent my heart from beating normally. I began to long for freedom from this prison environment I was in. I began to wonder if all families lived in such misery. *Surely there are happy, normal homes out there somewhere. What is normal, anyway? Are there healthy marriages? If so, what are they like? How does a healthy father relate to his children? Can a home filled with love, acceptance, happiness, and respect be possible?* I certainly didn't know the answers to any of these questions, but I was starving to know the truth.

It is important to remember that abusers are very crafty about where and when they abuse. They don't want to be seen or overheard; they don't want any witnesses. They want their vicious treatment to remain a secret. When I see a child being yelled at or physically jerked around in public, it always makes me wonder just how bad it is behind closed doors. From my own experience, I know that what was seen by others was not nearly as bad as what was done in private.

One Sunday morning on our way to church, it was just my husband and me. Something had made him angry, and he unleashed an abnormally harsh tirade on me. I don't recall that it ever had been this bad before. I felt as though I were a hostage in his car. The thought came to me more than once that when he came to a stoplight I would jump out. But I didn't have the courage. I knew he only would get angrier and might turn around and force me to ride with him. I believe the physical abuse would have begun at that time. Even if he had decided to continue to church without me, if someone else who also was headed to church had driven by and seen me walking on the main thoroughfare, he or she would have stopped to help. Then there would be no way I could hide how upset I was. And even if I managed to convince that person to let me continue walking, he or she would ask my husband about it later. He then would be angry with me because his image would be tarnished. Perfection was to be the image of our home at all times. Anything less would be addressed as intolerable and we would be told not to let it happen again. I never knew the full extent of what he would do, but the mere thought of it terrified me. I had no idea how badly it could escalate. To sit there and take it seemed easier than to cause a scene.

The way he was talking alarmed me. There was such an oppressive, demonic heaviness in the car. I felt as though I could suffocate. I often wonder if we hadn't been expected at church if he would have taken me to some remote location and killed me. It may sound bizarre to say that, but that's what I felt as I sat in the car listening to his verbal barrage.

After he parked the car at church, he put his "public" face on and proceeded to greet people as though nothing were wrong. I sat there in stunned silence. The man whom I once had loved, had chosen to marry, had given myself to, and had children with, now had revealed through his actions what a complete metamorphosis he had undergone.

At the time, I didn't know enough to put a label on it, but he had verbally and emotionally abused me. I tried to process all of the junk he just had unloaded on me. Please understand this was not an argument between us. He told me how something I had done (I can't even recall what it was all about) was inexcusable and that I was never to do that again. He then went into one of his speeches about how a wife is to be submissive at all times. Yet in this instance, there was a source of evil power behind it that I'd never felt before. I wonder if, at that time, he broke my spirit, or came close to it.

As I sat there in the car, I should have decided to cut and run. I didn't. I sat frozen in my seat, trying desperately to process what had just happened. This was more than just the emotional black eye I'd gotten in the past. My entire being had been emotionally beaten. I now felt blackened and bloodied. I couldn't believe it had come to this. It had happened so gradually, and I now understood the frog that slowly had been boiled to death, never knowing what had happened. I was severely scalded and incapable of getting myself out. I felt condemned to die in this increasingly volatile relationship. My mind was frozen in fear. I couldn't think clearly. I didn't know what to do. My mind raced in several directions at once.

I contemplated using my set of keys and driving away in his car. The question was: where would I go? To leave permanently seemed like a fantasyland of impossibility. Besides, he'd told me I never could hold down a full-time job and provide for myself. So that option was merely a dream. To go there in my mind was a waste of time. I had to come up with something else. I thought about just going back home. He would have been more than livid to find that his beloved car wasn't in the parking lot and he had no way home. What could happen once he came home terrified me. You see, his image would be tarnished because his wife had taken off and left him stranded. His image was his only security.

I then thought about calling one of my sons to come to pick me up. I knew they would protect me. Yet my mothering heart ached at the thought of getting them involved. I knew without a doubt that they would put a stop to this. However, I had no cell phone. And to go to the retail store just two buildings over and make a phone call seemed to be such a final act. The thought of what could take place after that terrified me. The only other thing I could think of was to go to the church and use the phone. My face could hide the turmoil no longer, so I knew people would ask me what was wrong and then approach my husband later. With so many people already there, I would not be able to have a private conversation on the phone.

Someone would overhear my call for a ride. Word would still get back to my husband, and it would be a very ugly situation. I was caught up in a whirlpool of confusion. I didn't know what to do.

The thought popped into my head just to drive away and that the destination would come to my mind as I drove. I didn't trust myself. If I began to drive away from him, I knew I'd never stop. There were still people in the car next to me. That stopped all possibility of my being able to process any of this. Keeping up the image was vital to my well-being and survival. I knew they would wonder why I just sat there. I busied myself with looking as though I was occupied with something in the car. I considered staying in the car until church was over, but that would raise questions from people at church, too. I thought about going to a nearby retail store and waiting in the parking lot until I saw people coming out of the church and then going back and picking him up. I found a reason to talk myself out of each option I came up with. The ideas either were flawed or I lacked the courage to carry them out.

Then a couple arrived who had spent hours counseling us during our separation. They parked closely to us. The wife was looking at me as though she would come over to see why I was sitting in the car alone. That made my decision for me. I didn't want to talk to her about this. Experience told me that she would side with my husband. I gathered my things and forced myself to walk inside. I felt as though the weight of the world was sitting on me. I tried to think of a place where I could hide from people while church was going on and then slip back outside to wait in the car, but I kept seeing one person after another. This was not going to work. I had no choice but to go through the motions numbly. There was a searing pain in the pit of my stomach that would not stop. I felt so trapped. I saw no way out. That event was a real turning point in our relationship. It was the beginning of the end.

The drive home was suffocating. My husband acted triumphant. He had won. He had beaten me down even more. I felt as though I were a worthless piece of slimy trash. I recall moving mechanically through life, trying to process it all but being unable to. My self-esteem had been obliterated, blown to bits by the explosiveness of his words and the oppression of the evil presence I'd felt in the car. My security was rattled to the core. My ambitions were completely squelched.

Often when I look back on that event, I can see clearly what I should have done. I just should have driven away. As the minutes clicked by, some plan, any plan, would have taken shape. This would have been a good time to have gone home; thrown a sheet on the floor; put legal documents, valuables, and necessities inside it; and left permanently. Anything else would have been better than for me to have walked into the church. Anything else would have turned the tables and been a new beginning for me becoming a stronger person. Looking back, my decision simply empowered my husband all the more, and he knew it. When he saw me later in church, he knew he had won. So did I. He felt vindicated. I felt defeated and hopeless. I had stayed too long in this farce of a marriage. We were nothing more than hostile roommates who also happened to be bed partners.

I began to beg God to allow someone to overhear how my husband talked to me. I desperately pleaded for weeks. The way God chose to answer that prayer was not what I would have chosen. One night I became violently ill with the flu. When either my husband or I was sick, I would sleep on the couch so that the other person would not catch the virus. It also gave me a break from him. It was a measure of freedom inside of my prison. This time, after about three nights of my sleeping on the couch, he'd had enough. Even though my husband already had gone to bed, he came back out to see when I was coming to bed. When he found I was already on the couch, he was furious. The traditional lecture that "a wife belongs in bed with her husband and nowhere else" began, as did the rest of his usual speech. This was nothing compared to what I had heard in the car; although the intense, unearthly oppression once again was thick in the room.

I was used to this scenario. I began to play my usual coping game. Since I knew this speech so well, I could anticipate what would be said. As he began, I ran ahead of him mentally and waited for his next point. When it

came, as I knew it would, I secretly laughed.
Then I anticipated what would come next.
When it did, I chuckled to myself again. This
continued until he was done. He angrily left and
returned to bed.

    Although I had been 100% accurate
with my coping game, it did not mean that what
he said had not affected me. It had. My heart
cried out in agony. So many emotions tumbled
through me. I felt so scared, angry, betrayed,
hurt, overwhelmed, and confused. My thoughts
were like the vortex of a powerful tornado,
endlessly spinning. I was in crisis, yet not aware
of it. All I knew was that my mind wouldn't
settle down. My thoughts simply would not rest
on any one thing; they chaotically raced in
circles. Our children had no idea just how bad
things were. I longed to run to one of them, but
that seemed so juvenile. A child is not supposed
to protect his or her mother. Our sons were now
seventeen and nineteen, men in their own rights.
I could have gone to them, and they would have
taken care of things, but it all seemed so bizarre.
I dismissed that thought as I always did. I felt
hopeless. I cried out to God for help.

Then I heard the sound of a door. I froze. It was my youngest son. He came out and sat in the same spot where his father just had been. He said, "Mom, I want you to know I just overheard what Dad said to you. *No one* should ever be talked to that way!" Finally, someone had overheard! My prayer had been answered! I reassured him that what he had heard was not the worst. He went on to say that regardless of that, it was still inexcusable. He told me he was going to sleep all night in the living room on the other couch. He repeatedly told me that I never again would have to be alone with my husband. The relief that washed over me was indescribable. I no longer had to carry this weight alone. I had help! Even though I was afraid of the repercussions of his father, I knew things would improve. I also knew that my eldest son would join him in protecting me.

My youngest son made me promise that if I heard his dad come out of the bedroom, I was going to wake him up so he could intervene if necessary. He said he was going to talk to his father the next night after he came home and confront him as to what he had overheard. He said, "Mom, I'm going to make sure he *never* talks like that to you again! There's no excuse for that." He told me he could feel the demonic presence so heavily while his father talked to me that the hairs stood up on his arms. So that wasn't my imagination either. The confirmation was soothing. I finally felt as though I was going to be taken care of!

Despite the incredible tension that was in our home and my fear of the future, I slept fairly well. That night was another turning point for me. Emotionally, my bags were packed. A few more events would have to transpire before I was out the door, but that day was coming closer all the time.

The next morning, my son was true to his word. As his father got up to get ready for work, he watched the proceedings like a hawk. I was needed in the kitchen. My husband came out to tell me what I was to do. Our son wasn't far behind him. When asked what he was doing in there, our teenager boldly told his father that due to what he had overheard the previous night, his father had lost the privilege of being alone with me.

My husband's sharp retort to him was, "What were you doing listening in on a private conversation? You can't tell me whether I can be alone with my wife or not."

My courageous defender again replied that his father had lost that privilege because of the way he had talked to me.

Again, the controlling reply was, "I'm your father, and I can talk any way I want to. She's my wife, and that's none of your business."

Our son's reply was, "No, you will not treat *my mother* like that. We'll talk more tonight. I have more than that I want to talk to you about."

"We'll see about that. I don't have to talk to you if I don't want to," was my husband's retort.

"We *will* have a talk tonight," were my son's last words.

WHIRLWIND

For You are my hiding place; You protect me from trouble. (Psalm 32:7 NLT)

I'll never forget that night as long as I live. Our youngest son sat down in the living room with his father and took charge. He would not allow my husband to talk but calmly began to say all that had been stirring inside him. I was so very proud of him. This lasted for probably an hour and a half if not more. I was so impressed. I'd never seen our son like that. He left no stone unturned; he covered each and every topic thoroughly. When he was done, my husband had nothing to say. Truly, there was nothing left to say. It had all been said.

Our eldest son found out what had transpired and told me he was more than willing to sleep on the couch so I could sleep on his bed with the door locked. Still not seeing the seriousness of it all, I thanked him but said "no." He made sure I knew that I could knock on his door any time I needed help. It meant so much. His willingness to protect me touched a deep place in my heart. I felt protected and cared for by what both of my sons were doing.

Yet it felt so backward to have our sons protecting me from their own father. It was all so twisted; it made no sense. Looking back on it now, just about everything in our lives was twisted. And I was growing increasingly terrified of what life would be like for me after both of our sons were out of the house. Not long after all this, one of our children came to me and said, "Mom, it's time for you to leave. I'm sick of seeing you have to live like this. Dad's never going to change. You need to go."

    This same person had approached me about two months prior and asked when I was going to serve my husband with divorce papers. My reply then had been, "I appreciate where you're coming from, but when I married your father, it was for life." This time, however, was different. I still believed that marriage was for life, but my circumstances had changed. I now was willing to consider what just had been said to me.

    I did not trust my judgment, so I called some trusted friends to ask them to pray with me about this. Some of them had no idea what had been going on; yet I called them because I knew that I could trust them. They proved me right. Some of them were horrified at the thought of me leaving, but they didn't let me know that then. These were close friendships that had been formed. I had known some of these people since I was a teenager. It truly was beyond their comprehension what it would be like without me close by. Others felt concerned, as I did, as to what the future would hold for me. They agreed to pray with me about it. The whole thing seemed so radical. I could not grasp that leaving my husband of over twenty years was truly God's will for me. Weren't those vows for life? I erroneously had been taught that you stay with your spouse no matter what, even if they physically abuse you. Yet I was willing to leave if that was the right thing. My heart began to change over the days that followed. The Lord made it clear that I was to go.

    Saying what seemed to be a final goodbye to precious friends was gut-wrenching. My heart felt as though it would break with each person I talked to. Each one had become like family to me. I'll never forget one dear lady, who, at the time, was an acquaintance. I had taken some items over to her house to drop them off before I left town. I was hoping I could leave them undetected on her front porch. My heart was very heavy as I turned and walked down her front steps and back to my car. The Lord made sure she saw me. I heard her call my name. Now my heavy heart dropped to my feet. What would I say to her? How could I tell her what my plans were?

As I came back up the steps, she asked why I didn't knock. I knew I had to be honest with her. I told her I was hoping she wouldn't see me. She instantly knew and shocked me by asking if I was leaving. I could only nod my head as tears coursed down my cheeks. With her position as a pastor's wife, I knew I could trust her. My story tumbled out. She hugged me and said she would miss me greatly, and definitely would be praying for me. I was blown away that she agreed that I needed to leave. As beaten down as I had become through the years, each piece of confirmation that I was doing the right thing was a rich blessing. This time as I descended her steps, my heart was a little lighter, as my load was now shared by my dear friend. She has remained in contact with me through the years, and I treasure her friendship.

Other friends have only recently told me how devastated they were that I was leaving. They kept their true feelings from me, as they knew I needed to leave. Their selfless actions may have spared my life. Had they shared their hearts with me, I may have stayed, but I doubt it. Life at home had become more than miserable. It was downright frightening.

My stepsister was the only extended family member who knew I was leaving. She and I had finally developed a close relationship. I didn't dare say a word to any other relatives. I knew who I could trust and who I couldn't. That kind of news most likely would have gotten back to my husband. (I will interject for clarification that I knew I could trust my sister, but she was living out of town by then.)

I began going through everything I owned, trying to decide what I would need to live on my own. I packed these things and hid the boxes so that they were ready to go. Income tax papers were copied, and my social security card and the title to my car were put with them. My driver's license and other important documents were kept close at hand, in case I needed to leave earlier than I anticipated. I should have kept a backpack ready with a couple of changes of clothes, a toothbrush, toothpaste, a hairbrush, feminine supplies, etc., but I didn't. Every family heirloom from my side of the family was put in a separate place for me to have in my new place, wherever that would be. Clothes, dishes, linens, and so much more would be needed to set up a new household. For days I sorted and tucked each item away in a safe place. The thought of being free was more than I could comprehend, but it also was very scary. Remember, it had been put into my head that I wasn't capable of making it on my own and that I never would be able to work full-time. Fears and plans swirled unceasingly in my head.

    For years my husband had been controlling with the financial gifts I received from my family. He expected me to use each present as he directed, usually to pay the bills. After years of this, I'd had enough. I had gone to the bank and opened a savings account in my name. For months I'd trembled with fear at what it would be like when the truth of what I had done was discovered. I still recall the terrifying moment when my husband found out.

He knew I had been given a check and powerfully "suggested" it would come in handy to pay a bill. Terrified, but trying to come across as strong, I told him I already had put it into my savings account. He was furious. He asked when I had opened my own account. Becoming more afraid, but not wanting him to know, I assertively raised my voice and let him know that the money had been given to me, not to the family. I said I was tired of him taking what was mine. I told him it had gotten so bad that my folks had begun to make out the checks with only my name on them, as they had become somewhat aware of what he was doing. That stopped the conversation, as he knew that I was right.

From that moment on, I heard comments about how spouses should not have separate bank accounts. Fear struck me with each comment. I struggled with guilt. Eventually, though, I saw that I had operated with courageous wisdom, as that small amount of money was all that I had to live on after I left him. Since he had this account number with our income tax papers, I knew I needed a new account before I left. If I didn't get one, I knew he would attempt to have an unsuspecting bank employee tell him where the latest transactions were done in an attempt to locate me after I left him. In so many ways, he was as sly as a snake. I had to be so careful to cover every possibility of a trail. I went to the bank and had my savings account closed down and a new one opened up so my husband would not have an account number. With my daughter's permission, I used her address so that he would not have access to any of my information. While my husband was away on a business trip, my wonderfully supportive children helped me go through the house. One of them had a place that had been set aside for storage of my things. This child had arranged it over two months prior, seeing what was inevitable. I was relieved someone had because I couldn't even see my hand in front of my face. Yet even with all these preparations, there was still one thing left. I needed to know when I was to leave.

In just a few days I had an appointment to see a psychologist for the first in a series of free visits through my husband's employer. During that first visit, I gave a condensed version of our marriage. The psychologist stopped me after about twenty minutes and asked me why I was still there. I already had been crying, but now I began to sob, "Because I've been waiting for you to ask me that question." Without knowing it, I was waiting for someone with experience to agree that I needed to get out of that toxic situation. Almost immediately, I felt that peaceful release from God; the time was right to leave. I knew deep down inside that the path ahead of me had been made clear, even though I couldn't see beyond my own nose. It was very scary, yet I knew God was watching over me. The psychologist asked if I knew where I was going. I said I did, but that I wasn't going to tell him so that my husband couldn't get it out of him; even in a court of law, he would be telling the truth that he had no idea where I was headed. He agreed.

The next morning after my husband had left for work, I began to assemble what I would take. I made sure to bundle up my medical and dental insurance cards, as well as the keys to the church and our house. I carefully placed them where he put his keys each night when he came home. I didn't want to be accused of anything in the future. I also wanted to convey that this was final. I had contemplated leaving a note. However, I knew that no matter what I said, it would be misconstrued and probably used against me.

    I checked more than once in each room and closet to be sure I had everything before I left. I then used my long-distance calling card to call the women's shelter where I would be staying. That way, their phone number, and location would not show up on the long-distance bill for our home phone. I knew I could not take the chance of leaving any trail that would lead my husband to me. I was confident now that leaving him was the right thing to do, but I did not understand the whole picture. That would come with time. As I have stated before, the volunteer who answered the phone told me that they didn't have a place for me to stay. Fear and dismay washed over me. How could this be? I knew this was the right time to go. Going against my nature, I became aggressive and said I could not wait any longer, and that I needed to leave that day. She slightly changed her tone and said for me to come. As if I didn't have enough worries whirling through my mind, I now had another to fight against—*where will I stay once I arrive?* I simply could not try to sort it all out now. I needed to go. Jesus would provide a safe place for me to stay.

As I headed out to the garage for the last time, I made a pit stop at the trash can to leave my negligees. I never would have to wear them again for anybody. Instead, they were going to rot in the town dump. It was the only thing close to a chuckle I'd had for a long time. It gave me such a sense of power to do that. I truly didn't care if my husband found them when he went to do trash. I kind of hoped he would. To me, it was a sign of finality to this whole farce of a marriage. I knew it would convey the same message to him if he found them. I even told my teenaged son not to move them or put anything else on top of them, as I wanted his father to see them as another sign of finality.

After a very emotional good-bye, I set out on what would be the most dramatic transformation my life had seen to date. Now that I was gone from my husband's clutches, I was more terrified than I ever had been before. His strong ties with four law enforcement agencies could lead him directly to me. For years I did all I could to stay out of reach of the law or of being discovered, whatever that might mean in any given situation. I knew I would have to stay one step ahead of him. One slip on my part would cause me to become his prey in this horrid game of cat and mouse I had entered into. Just the thought of getting back in his hands after leaving brought extreme panic. I knew the physical abuse would begin. His anger rarely surfaced. He was extremely proud that he could so stringently control it. Yet instinctively, I knew he would begin to batter me, and that ultimately, my very life would be in danger. I never had been able to voice that to anyone, as it sounded so bizarre. Deep down, though, I knew it to be true.

As I fled from my home, my children, my grandson, my precious mother, and my loving and supportive friends, the focus constantly bounced from the long road ahead of me to my rearview mirror. The fear that gripped me was that of seeing flashing lights behind me. Any run-in with the law could be easily discovered by my husband, and he would have a lead as to where I was headed. I couldn't afford a single mistake. It kept me constantly on my toes. There was no doubt in my mind that my survival depended on my listening to the Lord's leading. If I would ask for His direction consistently, His wisdom would keep me advanced beyond my husband's reach. The adrenaline was coursing through my body like never before.

Every thought of the future was so frightening. I was headed on a journey longer than I ever had driven before, to a location I never had driven to, operating a vehicle with an oil leak, to stay with people I didn't know—and that was *if* they even found a place for me to stay. I had no job in sight, no medical insurance, and only a small amount of money to live on. I prayed I wouldn't have an accident, as the car insurance was in both his name and mine. Any collision report would give a location, which could put him on my trail. There were so many negatives and so much uncertainty in my future. I seemed to be in a constant state of panic. I prayed constantly for wisdom to focus on the priority for each moment.

I stopped at least two times to allow the car to cool down so that I could check the oil. That was always a worry. If I had a problem with the car, who could I trust to work on it? I was all too aware of how mechanics take advantage of women. *Will my meager savings be enough to pay for a repair? If that takes all of my money, what will I live on once I arrive? How can I pay for an apartment if all my funds get spent on the car?*

Since I never had driven for that length of time, I wasn't sure how I would make it. The time seemed to go on and on. Thankfully, I was prepared with a variety of things to listen to. More than three hours had passed since I left before I saw the first road sign with the name of the city where I was headed. What a relief! Although I still had quite a distance to go, I briefly smiled at the joy of it all. So far, I was getting away successfully! A fresh start in life seemed to be a little more of a possibility. With each sign that said how much closer I was to my new home, I choked back tears of joy. As I finally pulled into town, some of the weight lifted from my shoulders. The fear was not totally gone, but I sensed the peace and safety of this new place.

UNTANGLING

> *...calamity overtakes you like a storm
> ...disaster engulfs you like a cyclone, and
> anguish and distress overwhelm you.
> (Proverbs 1:27 NLT)*

As I arrived at the shelter, I found that it was a rather unusual setup. I had to walk into a public place of business. I began a practice that was to become customary: I fearfully scanned each face to see if anyone was there that I knew. Every face was a stranger. I momentarily could breathe a little more easily. I had reason to be afraid of being spotted in public by mutual friends who lived in this area. Although they were wonderful people, I felt certain that they immediately would call my husband to alert him as to where I was. Their innocent hearts would be in the right place, as they would want to see our marriage reconciled. But there would be no reuniting of this husband and wife. That much I was sure of.

Because I was so tense when I arrived, every minute seemed to last an hour. It felt like it was such a long time before I had a solid answer about my being able to stay at the shelter. Even more time elapsed before I was directed to my room. Before I could have a key, I had to sign a form that I agreed I would not have any men in my room and that I would not divulge to anyone where I was staying. I understood not telling my location, but my initial thought was, *What are they thinking? Who would want a man in their room after they'd just left their abuser?* I soon learned that this is common. The national average is that a woman will return to her abuser six to eight times before she leaves him for good. She either calls him to tell him where she is, or she will call another man. But I'd had enough of men. They didn't have to worry about me. Men were something I was done with.

I parked the car so that it was not too visible from the road. No one was there to help me unload the car, so I did it by myself. Even that was scary, as I almost expected to see my husband or a police officer pull up next to my car. Each time I had a load ready to go into my room, I made sure the car was securely locked. My eyes continued to scan the traffic and the parking lot. I finally had all my possessions safely inside my new room. I locked the door behind me and felt as though I now could collapse. I no longer had to look the part of a normal woman; I could dissolve into tears. A relief washed over me like I never had known before. I was safe! I had escaped! It seemed surreal. Hopefully, my husband had no idea where I was.

I called the only other person I knew in this unfamiliar town. She knew I was coming. She'd had many people praying for me for weeks. They also had been praying for me that I would have a safe trip. The shelter had permitted me to let her know where I was staying. It wasn't long before she was at my door. It was so incredible to see her, to be able to hug her. It was a confirmation that this was not just a dream. Here was someone I knew. It was reality; I was free! We went out to eat for supper. I fearfully checked each face in the restaurant to see if there was a familiar one in the small crowd. Once again, I could breathe easily. Each time I heard someone come in, I worried it might be the law after me. My husband's close contacts with those four different law enforcement agencies gave me cause to be very afraid. My friend sat facing the door so that I didn't have to look each time it opened. We talked for the longest time. It was wonderful to unload on someone who knew me and my situation and was so concerned about every detail of what had transpired in less than thirty hours.

I slept better that night than I had in a very long time. The next morning, as I stepped outside, I fearfully scanned the cars in the parking lot, as well as the traffic going by. I saw nothing that looked familiar. Even temporary relief was nice. I headed to breakfast. After that, I was to meet with the director of the shelter for an entrance interview. Little did I know that the interview would not occur for another twenty-four hours. Instead, God had plans for me to stay right where I was so that I could be there when an unexpected phone call came for me.

As I sat and waited for hours, I was very glad I had brought my folder and writing paper. I knew I had to sort out my whirlwind mind. I jotted down ideas of what needed to be done to be on my own. I knew looking for a job was the top priority. After that, I needed to find a one-bedroom apartment to rent. It would depend on my income, but I wondered if I would be able to have a phone, cable, or the internet. That reminded me that I wanted to inquire about whether or not I could be traced if I had any of those services. I put that down as a question I needed an answer to.

I soon decided that if my husband could find me if I signed up for any of those services, then maybe I should change my name. My head began to spin with possible names. *What will I use for my last name? I certainly don't want to take my maiden name back. I want no connection to my father whatsoever. I love my first name. How can I give that up? Once I start working, if I use my new name, I wouldn't answer to that because it would be something I wasn't used to. What hoops would I have to jump through to change my name? How much does that cost? How would I get a new Social Security card with my new name on it? Would my Social Security number be different? My husband of over twenty years had my Social Security number memorized. Could this be handled like the Victim Witness Protection Program?* This all began to sound like a poorly-written novel. What was I thinking? I needed to get a grip and get some concrete steps lined out.

As my thoughts continued, I wondered about so many things. *Where is the cheapest place to get groceries? Who is a good doctor in case I need one? I have dental problems; what dentist should I go to? How will I pay for it? If my car breaks down, who should I call for a tow? Where should I have it towed to? What mechanics should I use if I need to get my car repaired? Will I be able to trust them, or will they take advantage of me? How can I afford it?* Mentally, I calculated each expense as it flashed through my overwrought mind. I saw my savings becoming more depleted by the minute. *How can the little money I have possibly be enough to help me get set up in my own place? Where will I go to get electricity and water turned on in my name?* That would depend on where I lived. I wrote those questions on the paper with the apartment issues.

There they were again, the constantly pressing money worries. Even as I loosely calculated the figures, I didn't see how my funds would stretch to pay for everything. I *had* to find a job. I wondered: *How much is the pay around here? What kind of a job can I get? Can I hold onto a full-time job? Am I physically able to handle working forty hours a week? How will I answer the inevitable questions of why I moved here? Will people get nosey? I heard that people in this area are helpful, but will they assist me if I need it? Can I really trust anyone? I didn't like the volunteer at the shelter and didn't know if I could trust her. What will the director be like? Is there counseling available?* I knew I would need someone to help me sort through my tangled mess. I scribbled that question on the list to ask the director. My mind continued to swirl unceasingly for hours. It seemed I couldn't shut it off.

Long after I had eaten lunch, I still was sitting there waiting. Then the phone rang. The volunteer I didn't like said the phone call was for me. I froze. *Who knows I am here?* I found my tongue and asked her who was calling for me. She said it was the director. Slightly relieved, I made my way to the phone. Unexpectedly, the director asked if I had a certain job skill. I did. She then said that there was a position open and asked if I could go for an interview in twenty minutes. Startled, I tried to get my overworked mind to focus. I had no prior commitments. So, I went.

When I arrived, the general manager was so kind. She was aware that I was a newcomer to the shelter. During the interview, she inquired about my skills and informed me about the job requirements. When she asked if I was interested, I was speechless. The last thing I expected was to be offered a job! I didn't know how to answer. My otherwise nonstop thoughts were finally at a dead standstill. I eventually sputtered out that I guessed I was.

She asked if there was any reason I would not be able to take it. I couldn't think of a thing. She offered me the job. I sent up a shotgun prayer, asking the Lord if I was supposed to take this job. No answer came. I silently asked God again what I should do. No answer. Not knowing what else to do, I eventually was able to get out a hesitant reply that I would accept the job. Then before I left her office, I was able to gather my wits about me and thank her.

Looking back, I wonder what that general manager thought. I wonder if she ever questioned her decision to hire me. I know now that I did not do well in her office. It's a wonder she even offered me the job.

As I exited the building, I tried to walk with as much grace as I could muster. It wasn't much; I all but fell into the seat of my car. After I shut the door, I threw both arms across the steering wheel and laid my head on it. I said, "Lord, I don't have a clue if what I just did was the right thing or not. If You don't want me to work here, then I need You to drop another job in my lap. Until you do, I'm just going to go on with this one. Thank You for what just happened. I'm amazed, God! Thank You!"

UNTANGLING

Since I was to begin work early the next morning, I knew I needed to get right back to the shelter and see what my next step would be. Before I left the parking lot, I looked at my watch. I could hardly believe my eyes. It hadn't even been twenty-four hours since I arrived in town, and I already had a job! I hadn't even had a chance to look for work, and here the Lord already had provided for me in such an incredible way! I didn't even have a résumé to bring to the interview, but I was now employed! If I had been out looking for work, I would have missed the phone call, and possibly have missed out on this opportunity. I was learning about trusting God in a new way. I had no idea what a huge blessing I was in for.

My new job proved to be such an incredible gift to me from the Lord. Most of the employees I worked with were young, energetic, and perpetually happy. No two days were ever alike, so I had no chance of becoming bored. My mind was able to be occupied with positive things in a fun atmosphere. This was just what I needed. My boss even became a dear friend. We had the common bond of having left an abusive husband. This is a sisterhood one never signs up for, but it can create an instant bond, as it did with us.

I worked forty to fifty-five hours a week. The overtime was just what I needed to help pay for the things I needed to set up an apartment and for numerous future car repairs. However, working that many hours proved to be a handicap of sorts. I had not anticipated how time-consuming it would be to get arrangements made to move, get utilities turned on, and begin to set up my new life. I was determined not to let any of this discourage me. I knew I had done the right thing in leaving my husband. I had no doubts about that. I was positive God had given this job to me. So I worked feverishly, even on my days off, to move my life forward.

One of the first afternoons I had off, I was at the shelter and decided it was time to call my sister and let her know what had happened. Although surprised, she gave me her full support. I knew her pledge of confidentiality was one I could trust. She had trusted me in a similar situation she had gone through several years before.

UNTANGLING

God began to direct my steps in a most unusual way. Especially during the next several months, each time a new step needed to be made, it seemed that most of the important people around me gave the same advice without knowing I already was contemplating that action. It was as though they all had talked among themselves as to what my next plan of action should be, yet none of them knew each other. I knew the Lord was giving me direction through them. That was an important lesson for me, to learn to listen to others. My life was moving at such a rapid pace. I was still in crisis. I had many huge, life-changing decisions to make, and others were able to see much-needed direction better than I was. Their counsel was priceless.

It wasn't long before I was able to begin getting counseling. I was so very grateful. Before I left my husband, I began to ask God to please send someone qualified to the shelter where I would be staying, as I knew I desperately needed help sorting out my emotional garbage. I asked that if there wasn't anyone there to do that yet, He would draw that person there. When this counselor and I sat down to talk, I shared this with her. Amazingly, she had not begun working with the women until just days after I had prayed. I was so astounded, but I shouldn't have been; Jesus always has been faithful to meet my needs.

It was in that first session that I asked her if my husband could trace me if I signed up for the internet, cable, or a home phone once I moved. She checked into it and reported to me in my second session with her that, yes, I was traceable if I signed up for any of those services. That was all right. I would be content to live a very simple life.

One of my priorities was to obtain a post office box in a small town near where I lived. I had no idea how long I would be in the shelter or where I would live once I was able to live on my own. This proved to be one of the wisest choices I made. It not only gave me a permanent address but also it kept my physical address confidential. Also, my children could stay in contact with me, yet not know my location. Staying in touch with my children was vital for me. Yet for me to remain safe, they each put my name into their cell phones under a false name so that if their father obtained access to their phones, he could not locate my contact information. My mother did the same thing with my contact information once I rented the post office box. Until the day she died, she had all of my information in her address book where no one else would find it.

I even needed to be careful what I mailed to my mom, as I did not trust my husband not to look in their mailbox and take anything that was from me. Abusers can be so sly. It was a constant process of trying to be more than one step ahead of my husband. I felt maybe I was being paranoid, yet one of my sons voiced the same thought. His validation of my thoughts helped me in another baby step toward believing that maybe I was not the crazy one.

One fact that I found out almost a year later is that I should have faxed or sent a certified letter to the Postmaster of the town where I left. In it, I could have requested that all my mail be forwarded to my new address and that a change of address card *not be sent* to my former address. It's just another step I could have taken to protect myself had I known.

In the meantime, I had a problem with my car. The license plates would expire in a matter of days. I wanted to get tags in the new state I had moved to. This would be one less way my husband could look for me. As I thought about that, I knew he had access through the different law enforcement agencies to track the Vehicle Identification Number (VIN). Merely putting new tags on a car he already knew I had still would give him the ability to track me down. Also, my car was not very common, so it was easy to spot. I knew I had to trade in my car for another one. This way I would be a little more difficult to track down or spot in traffic. It seemed ridiculous to go to such lengths, but I knew it was necessary to try to hide from my husband. My sons agreed it would be wise, so I went to the car lot of a Christian man who came highly recommended. I will forever thank the Lord for what a gift he was to me.

Looking back, I have to chuckle when I think about what in the world the man must have thought he was getting into as I sat there and told my story. I'm sure it's not often a woman begins to cry while in his office. It only had been about two weeks since I'd made my frightening escape. I still was attempting to get out of the shelter and on my own. My emotions were running very high. Life was still very scary for me. I missed my children and grandson terribly. As I sat at the desk of this pleasant businessman, I did try to give him a condensed version of my story. Of course, the tears flowed as I told it between heavy sobs. Everything was not only still fresh in my mind, but I was still at a crisis point in my life.

The idea the man came up with blew me away. He told me he would take my car as a trade-in, and then he'd make sure it was taken to a car auction in another state. Many people from out of the country came there to buy vehicles and then drive them across the border. That way, if my husband looked up the VIN, it not only would not be in the state where I now lived, but also it very possibly could be out of the United States entirely.

Once I had my new vehicle, car insurance was another issue. I was not going to use the same company my husband had. It would be perfectly fitting for him to walk into the insurance office and ask for information as to my whereabouts. (Years later I found out he showed up at that office more than once and showed himself to be the unpredictable jerk I had known him to be.) I found a company with a good reputation for keeping customers' information very private. The car and insurance were two huge weights off my shoulders. Now I could move on to the next step.

I had to remove my husband as my primary life insurance beneficiary. Contacting the insurance company was risky. I couldn't think of anyone I could trust. Then I remembered one lady who was divorced. I knew she had gone through some really difficult situations with her ex-husband. I knew she was tough and could stand up to my husband if he crossed her path. I decided she would be the person I would try to contact. Fearfully, I used my long-distance calling card so my location was not traceable. As was typical during that time, I called from a pay phone, but each time she was on another line. I could not afford to take the chance of leaving the cell phone number my son had given me. Since I did not know the other employees, I had no reason to be able to trust them. After several attempts, I finally was able to reach her. She was more than helpful. She became a trustworthy friend who kept my address confidential. In record time, I received the paperwork to remove my husband as my primary beneficiary. Right there in the parking lot of the Post Office, I signed that paperwork and immediately mailed it back to her. We also arranged to have my monthly bill mailed to my stepsister's house. She then forwarded it to me. I, in turn, sent her the money so that she could pay the bill. These were a lot of extra steps, but worth it for my safety.

My husband did call my stepsister at least once, trying to get information as to where I was. Thankfully, she did not tell him a thing. I believe he thought I was staying either with her or with my biological sister, who lived near where he worked. That was fine with me, as it kept him away from where I was—at least for the time being.

After only a few days, I had a visitor. A friend and her husband already had planned their trip long before I left. Since none of us knew I would be there, it was unexpected, but it was a huge blessing to be able to see another friendly and familiar face. During our brief visit, I was able to surrender my wedding rings to her. She took them to a jeweler, who appraised them for me. She then kept them until I had a plan of what I was going to do with them. One thing I knew for sure, I no longer wanted to wear them. It was a joy to get them off my finger. I saw it as one more move in the right direction. Those unhealthy ties needed to be broken. With each step like this, I felt a new level of freedom.

Before trading in the car, I moved to another shelter in the area. I chose to move because I knew that I was costing the first shelter a lot of money. I never got a chance to find out exactly what they offered in the way of assistance since I was now working long hours. This new shelter not only had a refrigerator, stove, and dishes but also food stocked in the kitchen cabinets and freezer. I was choked up to see the thoughtful provisions that had been made. In the tiny bathroom, there was a supply of travel-size shampoo and conditioner, a toothbrush, toothpaste, a comb, feminine supplies, and so much more. While there, I was only able to attend a few group sessions, but they were so helpful. It was eye-opening to hear what other women had lived through and to see the common threads in each of our stories. More than once, it left me physically shaken, as I saw more clearly what I'd been through. It had a name: abuse. I was validated to feel the way I did. I *did* need to leave my husband. My confusion, fear, and shame made more sense. I was beginning to realize that maybe I wasn't crazy but wounded. This was a big step in the healing journey.

In one session, we must have talked about the different types of abuse (see the "Breaking It Down" section at the back of the book for more information). It seemed clear to me that what I had suffered most was emotional abuse. The advocate turned and looked at me, and with genuine care in her eyes said, "Emotional abuse is the hardest to recover from." I began to cry. It hit me so hard that I felt I needed to run to my cabin at the shelter and sob. But I didn't. I stayed for the rest of the session, but I left there very shaken.

This new shelter also had a wonderful staff. My new advocate willingly shredded business cards and paperwork for me. I was so afraid that my husband would have people looking for anything they could find with my former hometown information on it. I felt that would point them to me, and he would be alerted to my new whereabouts. One thing to note, I still am careful not to leave handwritten notes face-up in the car, as my handwriting could be recognized. It's amazing how cautious I still feel the need to be after more than 20 years of freedom. In an ordinary case, I don't believe I would feel this way. But his connections with the law gave me a reason to keep my eyes open. Thankfully, his family doesn't cause me any alarm.

While I was in this second shelter, my sister came to visit and brought me some treasured items that one of my sons had delivered to her. I wept to be able to have these things back in my possession. This was just one more thing in a growing list of things that showed me how the Lord was providing for me. His allowing me to have those special items once again also showed me His tender care.

For months after leaving my husband, many thoughts haunted me. In any given situation, I could hear his strong opinion being voiced in my mind, or if a problem arose that I had no idea how to handle, I would wonder how he would deal with it. I began to understand why so many women return to their abusers. They've never been allowed to make a decision or solve a problem, so they truly are at a loss to know how to function in that capacity. Another thing that continued to haunt me until recently was hearing his taunting when I would wring out my washcloth after a shower. He always loved to come behind me, wring it out again, and laugh at how much water was still left in it. This was his way of making a point of how much stronger he was. It was a constant reminder of his ability to overpower and belittle me. I still have to choose to laugh at that and remind myself that he may be stronger physically, but I'm free from his grasp because my God is more powerful than he is!

Within a matter of days, after I left him, my husband visited my mom and her husband. He returned a few days later to talk alone with my stepfather. The next time I spoke with my stepdad, he point-blank told me he didn't know who to believe. That pierced my heart. To me, it proved that I never had been family to him. It also told me that from one abuser to another, they not only spoke each other's language but also could identify with each other's logic. It hurt very deeply. It felt to me like I had taken a knife in the stomach.

Before our wedding, my husband had made subtle comments regarding my family members and close friends. Both my husband's body language and tone of voice made it clear that he did not approve of any of these individuals and that he did not want me to have contact with them. After a while, belittling remarks about each person became a common practice. He would be at least civil if not cordial when with them, but he would give his unsolicited editorial of them freely as soon as we were alone.

I can recall only one friendship that he succeeded in causing me to completely sever during that time. She was very dear to me, and I regret it to this day. Gratefully, I knew the rich value of a good comrade. Although I distanced myself from other friends, I never completely severed those ties, much to his disdain.

My husband also definitely did his best to keep me separated from my family. Of course, they had no idea. They were clueless about how he truly felt about them. He honestly couldn't stand any of them. I would have been in real trouble with him if I ever had said anything about how he felt or what was really going on. Plus, he was such a good actor and they were so undiscerning that I would not have been believed. It would have created more of a stink than I was willing to face. It never seemed worth the price. It simply was easier at the time to do what I could to keep peace in our home at all costs. It was ironic, though; the people he despised either took a neutral stand or sided with him.

I paid for my silence in the end, when I lost most of my family's support after leaving him. The way I chose to look at it was: it was their loss. I'm not being prideful; I merely see that they lost out by not believing the truth. The fact that they didn't believe me simply fits in with the statistics—the victim's family rarely supports him or her when they leave.

My poor mom didn't know what to think. All she knew was that her daughter was gone. Having lived under the same roof with her husband, I am sure she had a very difficult time processing my leaving. He didn't allow any other opinions in his house other than his.

The stepsister I was closest to stopped communicating with me. The other stepsister was patronizing and came across as insincere and belittling. I knew she and her husband strongly believed that a woman should stay, even with a physically abusive husband. I didn't trust either of them. They and at least one of their children have had some contact with him since I left. To this day, they have limited information as to how to contact me. It would be in character for them to give my ex-husband information about me.

One example regarding my stepfather's family stands out in my mind. My son was at the local ballpark and saw one of the step-family members. Several people were grouped together as they all talked. This family member had the gall to say he didn't know what was wrong with me and wondered out loud why I felt I had to leave as suddenly as I did. He went on to say that he recently had seen my husband and there was nothing wrong with him. My son was furious to have this person talking about his mom like that, especially in front of other people. But he opted to remain silent, as he knew if he opened his mouth, he would say something that he might later regret. It was one more piece of evidence to prove that I never belonged to my stepfather's family. That rejection was just one more dagger in my heart, as though I needed any more.

All of this has been very difficult to deal with. As I have processed it numerous times, I have chosen to forgive them. I do *not* want to carry bitterness into this new life I have begun. To be honest, it still hurts, but not like it did initially when I heard about the conversation that took place. Gratefully, I have been able to create a new "family" that listens to me, believes what I tell them, and fully supports me. They have been a much-needed lifeline when I have felt as though I was drowning in a violent whirlpool.

Another top priority for me was finding a church. I longed to be able to put down spiritual roots. I knew how important it was to be taught accurately from the Bible and to spend time with other people who also believe in having a relationship with Jesus. However, I had been deeply hurt by the pastor in the church my husband still attended. This caused me to approach this "church search" with a negative, distrusting eye for each pastor and his leadership. I didn't dare visit any churches of the same denomination as the one my husband still attended. With each church I did visit, I would not fill out a visitor card. I did not want to leave a trail of any kind, no matter where I went. I knew that if the Lord wanted me in that church, I would be able to trust at least some of the people with my contact information. Until then, I was not taking that chance. I had no idea what kind of a lengthy procedure this was to be.

For almost two years, I visited one church after another. Some I attended more than once to see if they were a fit for me or not. During this long period, there was a church that allowed me to attend a study they were doing. That was a blessing to be able to get good foundational teaching that was centered around the Bible. Because of what I had come out of, I was determined to commit only to the church God wanted me in. Only He knew which one was the right one for me. I continued to ask Jesus to direct me each week. I told Him over and over that I was not going to choose the one I wanted. There was no way I was going to trust my judgment. He needed to show me where He wanted to place me.

Finally, that day came, and it felt so good to be where I knew for certain that He wanted me. Yet my wounded spirit had a difficult time trusting others. The common questions from them as they wanted to become acquainted with me were met with my direct answers or with fear as I pulled away from them. My direct answers seemed to cause some to back away, as they didn't know what to do with me. The wise thing to do would have been to soften my answers. For example, when asked why I had relocated, my typical response was that I had left an abusive husband. I should have said I needed a fresh beginning in my life. Then as I got to know them better, I could have given them more of the hard facts.

I want to add here that when I donated to my church, I gave cash, even up to the day I initially wrote this book in 2011. I didn't feel it was wise to write a check when I first started going there. My husband knew one of the bank employees. Also, our divorce was not settled yet, and his attorney had access to my bank accounts. It is my opinion that he does not need to know any of my private information, including what church I attend, no matter how he would try to get that information now. Giving cash keeps it as private information.

Within the first few weeks after I left, I received three phone calls that still astound me to this day. In separate conversations, all three of our children expressed their relief that I had left. They all said that they fully believed their father would eventually have killed me if I had stayed. Deep down inside, I had known that for a long time, but I never could have admitted that to anyone, even myself. It was another way my husband's psychological abuse continued to plague me. To admit something of that magnitude would have sounded as though I were crazy. He wanted me to believe that I was. To have acknowledged that my life was in danger also would have meant I needed a game plan to escape, something I had not been ready to deal with yet. I knew when each of my children said the same thing, it was God's way of confirming to me that what I had known deep within was true.

DISCOVERIES

*I will instruct you and teach you in the
way you should go; I will counsel you
with My loving eye on you.
(Psalm 32:8 Today's NIV)*

Getting into a place of my own was an interesting process. I was able to use a phone at the shelter, but only for fifteen minutes at a time so that everyone could have a fair chance at making calls. To save minutes on my son's cell phone, I constantly kept a long-distance calling card on hand with plenty of minutes available. The next step was finding an available pay phone to call from. That was how I conducted the business of setting up an apartment and getting the utility companies called. It was also how I kept in touch with my family and friends. On those rare occasions when I needed to conduct business with someone in the town where my husband lived, I made sure I used a pay phone that was nowhere near where I lived. I didn't feel I could be too careful, since I wasn't sure whether my location could be traced or not. I finally bought a collapsible lawn chair that I carried in the trunk of my car so that I could sit while I was on the phone. I'm sure it looked very odd, but I had gotten to the point that I didn't care what people thought. Since I was on my feet most of the forty-plus hours a week at my job, I needed to sit down to relieve my back pain.

I unexpectedly received a call one day while I was at work. In the voicemail, my son said that several of my things would be delivered to me that night. This was an incredible gift! I had no idea what items they were going to be, but I was glad to be able to see my son and his friend. By the description of some of what they were bringing, I knew that I had no place to store the things at the shelter. And because I had no idea they were coming, I hadn't arranged for a storage unit ahead of time. It was after dark before we were able to find one and get everything moved in. My son and his friend needed to turn right around and drive back, so it was a precious, yet short visit.

When my son arrived back home, he had been locked out of the house. The friend who had come with him allowed him to stay the night with him. The next day, my husband told our son he was kicking him out of the house. He did this to punish our son because he had brought my personal possessions to me. He had the nerve to accuse him of being a traitor and a thief and said, "I should have you arrested for stealing."

Now our seventeen-year-old son had no place to live. He didn't know what he was going to do, but he was willing to sleep in his car and shower at the local gym, where the employees knew him. Thankfully, some family members allowed him to stay with them. When that proved to be inconvenient, one of my son's coaches offered him a room in his basement. I will be forever grateful to that single man for taking him in. While my son was staying there, the man married; yet he and his new wife were firmly committed to my son.

Just one month after I left my husband, I was able to move into my own apartment (move number nineteen). I was so grateful to have help with the security deposit and rent from a local organization. The utilities had to be put in my name, so I knew this was just another step in learning to trust the Lord to protect me from being traced. I let each utility company know of my situation. They assured me that my husband would have no way of obtaining that information. My game plan was to pay my rent and utilities with money orders so that there would be no record of it in my checking account. I moved my belongings by myself one more time. It felt fantastic to have a place to call home once again. It was mine. I was paying for it with my hard-earned money from my full-time job. Even though it was cavernously empty, I loved it. I had no furniture, only boxes lined up against one wall. I didn't have a chair, table, or even a bed. But I was determined not to be discouraged.

I bought an air mattress to sleep on that first night. Then I set out to take care of some business before I began to put my things away. I sat on the floor and made a meticulous list of every item my son had brought me. I listed every item in detail. I had no idea if it would hold up in a court of law, but I knew I needed to do what I could in case my husband tried to accuse me of stealing. I was aware my husband would try every trick in the book to accuse my son of taking things that did not belong to me.

About two weeks later, I bought two plastic patio chairs and a matching patio coffee

DISCOVERIES

table. My aging body was grateful not to have to sit on the floor anymore. I was thankful my life was improving, no matter how little the progress was. In the next month, God graciously saw to it that I had three more deliveries of needed furniture and household goods.

Two months after kicking our youngest son out, my husband managed to have a gift delivered to our son. A letter accompanied the gift that said he had watched our son play ball even though our son had had no idea his father was there. My son and I both found this very eerie. Later on in the letter, it said, "…I still want to be your daddy. I am here for you." Yet nowhere was there an apology or reference to anything that previously had been spoken. It was signed, "Love, Dad." I was learning to read between the lines, but I still had so much to find out regarding abusers. One simple piece of information is that they are masters at pointing a finger in accusation, but rarely will they admit fault in a matter, much less apologize. Nonetheless, this episode rattled me, as well as my two sons.

About three months after I left, my husband kicked our eldest son out of the house as well. My heart ached for both of my sons. I longed to be able to be there for them. I was so glad we could stay in touch through both phone and mail. It was a lifeline for all of us.

After several months of sleeping on an air mattress, some friends delivered a couch and a loveseat to me. I no longer had to struggle to get up and down from the floor. It was wonderful! I also felt safe being back on a couch. It brought back memories of being able to sleep on the couch when either my husband or I was sick. Even then it had given me a safe, cocoon sensation, as there wasn't room for my husband to come and sleep there with me. Having this couch to sleep on once again created that secure feeling, knowing that there was only room for one person.

One issue I had to deal with was that I longed to be able to register to vote in my new home, yet I knew that I would be traceable if I did. Three times I went to see our county clerk to check and see if the law had changed. She was so very kind and patient to listen each time I went in to see her. After I missed a presidential

DISCOVERIES

primary, I knew I could not go through that agony again. Being able to vote is something I take very seriously. I finally made the hard choice: I went in to register to vote. Although it was scary to think of the prospect, I just couldn't sit back and allow others to elect people into positions of authority that would make decisions that would affect my life. Since then, I have heard of protection that is available in some states for voting, owning a home, and even testifying in court, without your physical address being made known.

I soon began to get phone calls on my son's cell phone which disturbed me. This went on for months. There was no pattern as to when the calls would come, but they were almost all alike. The male caller always asked for a person with a name similar to mine. It was a name that my husband knew I hated, yet it was so like my own that I would answer to it if caught off guard. As soon as I responded to the caller, he would hang up. I tried not to let this bother me. I suspected that my husband somehow had gotten the phone number and was harassing me. To this day, I still use the manufacturer's voicemail announcement on my phone so that my voice is not on there. And there are still times I will not answer a call when I don't recognize the number.

My fear of being spotted by friends, family, or even my husband was still very smothering during this time. I had two strong young men I knew from work accompany me for protection as I went for an eye exam in another town. Extended family members lived there. I had been informed that they had been given instructions to notify my husband or his brother if I was seen. I knew that they also would include information regarding who was with me, the car we were in, and license plates.

Each time I stepped out of my apartment, even if it was only to take my trash to the dumpster, I needed to be ever vigilant of my surroundings, the cars in the parking lot, and each person within my sight. It did not matter if they were in a vehicle or not. Each trip to the store was frightening for me. I looked at each face to see if anyone recognized me. Truly, I was terrified I would run into our mutual friends who lived about five miles from me. If they ever saw me, I still felt that in their innocence they would contact my husband. I

DISCOVERIES

could not afford for my hiding place to be uncovered. I desperately needed space to begin to heal and sort things out. Every time I got in my car, I felt I still had to be so careful not to do anything that would alert the law to pull me over. I had been told that there wasn't a single city or county law enforcement agency that was not corrupt in the new area where I lived. To me, that meant they would play right into my husband's hands and assist him with whatever information they could give him.

Fear, worry, and the grief of being so far from my children, grandson, mother, and friends constantly swirled in my head. Playing worship music and singing to Jesus was the only relief from all that seemed to weigh me down. I would worship the entire way to work. It was the only way I got through each day. Even though I loved my job and adored my co-workers, I still would feel depression trying to creep in. I became determined not to wallow in it. I had made up my mind that self-pity was not going to become a part of my life. When those moments would come, I would say, "Lord, I refuse to be depressed. You have done so much to take care of me. I'm so very grateful for the way You have helped me start a new life. Thank You!" Many times, the heaviness would leave. Those times when it didn't, I plowed through with the duties of my job, pushing away the negative thoughts and continuing to thank God for what He had done. One thing I did know was that it was emotionally healthy for me to be thankful for the new, wonderful things that were taking place in my life.

However, I knew I needed help sorting through all of the emotional garbage. It was obvious to me that I had more questions than answers. It truly was a necessity to process this confusing mess with someone skilled in dealing with issues like mine. The counselor I had been seeing had needed to withdraw her voluntary services to the shelter, but the Lord graciously saw to it that I regularly was able to see a woman who was not just a licensed counselor but also a psychologist. If that wasn't enough, in the two years I saw her, I never had to pay a dime!

I still recall our first session. Her gentle, caring nature helped put me more at ease. As she softly asked me to tell her my story, I began to cry. The pain and fear poured out as I attempted to give her a condensed version of what had taken place. She was such a good listener! I finally had a qualified person who would not only pay attention but also validate my need to leave my abusive husband. I truly don't know where I would be today if it were not for this amazing woman. She helped me sort through all the trash that had accumulated in my life and gain understanding from it. Our time together was such a learning process. I was like a slave who had gotten free from her master. Now I needed to learn how to live responsibly and unselfishly in my newfound freedom. Thankfully, she helped me through that as well.

In that first session, the counselor said that the longer I was away, the more of the truth I would see. She was so very accurate with that. Among other things, I began to see even more clearly just what a master my husband was at shifting the blame onto me. If I said our marriage was in trouble, it was my fault. According to him, he was doing everything I had asked him to do. He then would proceed to list those things to me as proof. If I commented about our financial troubles, that also was my fault. Life with him was very complicated. His ability to twist and distort the truth almost could convince me the sky was purple instead of azure blue.

Another thing I began to see was how he had projected things about himself onto me. During a "discussion," if I brought up the subject of how he had hurt me, he would turn the character flaw around on me. I desired to get emotionally healthy, so I would take his comment and look inside myself to see if what he had said was true. Even though I truly did not see it, I would take that label on as though it were mine. This was repeated over and over throughout the entire conversation. I was so confused before we even got to the final point. This game of mental abuse he played wore me down. I began to wonder if I was crazy, as he had intimated that I was. Yet repeatedly, my new counselor looked me square in the eyes and said, "I see no sign of any psychoses in you." Each time, the tears would pour down my face; sometimes I would sob when she said that. It was such a deep healing to be validated as normal, as well as to see his mental abuse for what it was.

DISCOVERIES

Due to several things I had told her, this precious psychologist soon confirmed that my husband was financially abusive. First of all, there was a failure to provide. He also complained about medical care costs for the children and me. Gas usage in our vehicles was scrutinized; unnecessary trips were punished with silence. If we were short of cash or gas in the car, the unnecessary trip was brought up as the reason. (Of course, if he ran low on gas before his next paycheck, the needed money appeared out of nowhere.) My out-of-town trips of just twenty or thirty minutes in one-way travel needed to be authorized first. After all, these could be considered "unnecessary." The bottom line for him was if I was out of gas or there was a problem, it was my fault for lack of judgment.

Then I had it confirmed that he also was emotionally abusive. One example of this was his desire for us always to account for our whereabouts. As I mentioned before, when he was employed in town, he would stop in during the day. Although it could be taken as just wanting to see us, it began to feel as though we were being checked on. After he began to work out of town, his frequent phone calls seemed to be designed to catch me off guard. If I did not answer, I later had to tell him where I was and what I was doing. This sense of control kept me on my toes, a reminder that I was not to leave the house unnecessarily. I felt stifled. I have no idea if I was able to keep this from the children or not. Eventually, I got to the place where I didn't care whether or not they were aware. They began to see their father for what he truly was, and they even grew bold enough to confront him without any prodding from me. Secretly, I was very proud of them. I was weary of the fantasy world he lived in, where he was the only true, wise one. It didn't take my children long to get to that point of weariness either.

One thing I've seen for sure is that eventually, you will become bitter at those you have allowed to oppress you. It's quite a process to work through. I was not able to get anywhere with this until I left my husband. Finally, I was able to forgive myself for allowing him to control me and for not standing up to him. I also eventually came to a place where I was able to forgive him, but that took a lot of time. If I'm not careful, I still can get over into the life-stealing position of anger and bitterness easily. However, I don't stay there for long anymore, as I've come to love peace. Now I seem to be entering a place where I'm becoming addicted to peace. I also enjoy the little daily gifts that being alive brings. For instance, as I've worked on this book, it has been my joy and delight to watch the artistry in the beautiful clouds outside my window. The woods outside my door are so restful to view, too. The birds cavorting on my balcony are delightful, and the flowers are fascinating in their color, texture, and delicate beauty.

When I first got my job, I knew it would be temporary. It was only to last for a little over eight months. Although that seemed to be an eternity at the time I was hired, it became clear that I needed to find a permanent job. I soon was able to find one. That meant that within four months of arriving in town, I had a permanent, full-time job. I would not be getting the overtime hours I had with the first job, so it was essentially a pay cut, even though the hourly wage was the same. This was a different type of job. I would be working alone most of the time. And although this job had benefits, which I didn't have before, I just wasn't sure if I had made the right decision in taking the job.

The duties of my new job proved to be much more difficult than I expected. I was working the graveyard shift four nights and then one day shift each week. The janitorial duties included cleaning the public restrooms on my hands and knees, as there was no mop. Then on the graveyard shift, I had to exit the building several times each night to clean and do security rounds on the entire property. I kept pepper spray in the same pocket at all times for easy access. I was not taking any chances. When I went on my rounds, it was in my hand, cocked, with my finger on the trigger.

Three months after I left my husband, I was informed that he was going on a "mystery" road trip. He said he knew where I was and that he had plans to enlist the help of the police to locate me. He had made the comment that I eventually would have to come out of hiding. I had reason to believe what my husband said was possible due to a piece of mail I had received regarding my new post office box. It

DISCOVERIES

seemed to elude that my husband may have received the information as well.

After I received the news about my husband's coming trip, I was talking to my advocate from the shelter and she asked how I was doing. I told her of my husband's plans as I choked back the tears. She offered to let me stay with them. I was amazed. She said their mission was to assist me with housing if I felt my safety was at risk. Overwhelmed with gratitude, I made plans to stay with them again during the weekend he was planning to be gone. This also was the first weekend I would be working alone at my new job. I was so afraid, yet I tried so hard to be brave. I stayed at the shelter for five days to be sure I wasn't at home alone if he was in town.

Before his possibly coming to town, I went by myself and talked directly to the sheriff, the police chief in my town, and a police detective in the neighboring city. I bluntly asked if he had contacted them. Of course, each answer was "no." I made sure they knew how he had used his local law enforcement connections to locate people in the past. Each face showed surprise. I also firmly let them know that I did not want any of my information given to him if he came to town. They assured me that they would not share it. Since I was not able to trust any of them, the only confidence I left with was that I assertively had made my point clear. This had been a huge step for a timid person like me. However, I felt compelled that it was necessary.

After all that, the whole thing turned out to be a bluff, as he ended up going on a fun excursion several hours away to see a friend. His mind games always had been exhausting. Although I was extremely relieved, I also wanted to collapse instantly and sleep for hours.

Just days after this momentous weekend, my youngest son came to live with me. Words cannot describe how incredible it was to have him at my side. Not long before he came, a friend had brought a twin bed from her own home. This was such an awesome provision for my son and me.

It wasn't long before my son found work. In fact, he ended up with two jobs. I was so proud of him; during one temporary stretch, he was working seventeen hours a day. I knew my fears of his father finding us were not ridiculous when my son would not give out his new cell phone number to people he knew from our former town since the phone had GPS built in. (That was a new feature then.) If his father had gotten his phone number, it could have led him to our apartment. My son would not take the chance of his father finding us. It helped to confirm that it was not my imagination or an overreaction for me to be so cautious.

Around this time, my daughter told me that my husband had grabbed our grandson, jerked him, and yelled at him. I never had seen him do that. He also began to treat our daughter as though she were me. He even called her by my nickname. These behavior changes and others I heard about concerned me greatly. I began to wonder just what he was capable of. However, I could not allow my mind to go there. That was too frightening.

As time went on, I continued to receive several reports of how my husband's behavior had changed, but the reports grew increasingly bizarre. I was beginning to think he was about to snap.

FREE TO SOAR

DIRECTIONS

For the Lord, the God of Israel, says: "I hate divorce and marital separation, and him who covers his garment [his wife] with violence. Therefore, keep a watch upon your spirit [that it may be controlled by My Spirit], that you deal not treacherously and faithlessly [with your marriage mate]. (Malachi 2:16 AMP)

I still struggled with the topic of divorce. Yet no one could tell me what I should do regarding divorce. How could God want me to do that? I began to have a little of the fog lift when my counselor said that this divorce would be due to mistreatment, and mistreatment grieves the Lord. Her statement came after several people had talked to me at random times, all saying the same thing; yet none of them even knew each other.

Then even my mother advised me that if for no other reason, I needed to get a divorce to protect myself legally. She knew my husband was more than irresponsible with money. I needed to protect myself from any debt he could incur. I couldn't believe what I was hearing. The last person I expected to get that kind of advice from was my mom. That helped me to make up my mind. It was time to file for divorce.

I found out later that my mother was exactly right, as my husband had incurred another debt after I left him. It was there in black and white in the divorce papers that were exchanged months later. He had been so kind as to include my name on the loan he had taken out.

For those of you who still struggle with the issue of divorce, let me add something here—another morsel for you to chew on. Just recently, I was talking with a co-worker who also had left an abusive husband. She, too, had wrestled with the same thing, as she'd also married for life. Until she found this scripture, she stayed with him; she wanted Biblical proof that God would give her permission to leave. She shared with me Malachi 2:16 from the Amplified Bible. Although it is quoted at the top of this chapter, I will include it here as well. It says, "For the Lord, the God of Israel, says: 'I hate divorce and marital separation, and him who covers his garment [his wife] with violence. Therefore, keep a watch upon your spirit [that it may be controlled by My Spirit] that you deal not treacherously and faithlessly [with your marriage mate].'" As you read the section entitled "Breaking It Down" at the back of this book, you will see several types of abuse defined and examples given. Each one comes under the title of "domestic violence." Take a look at that verse again. God says He hates the one who covers his wife with violence.

Psalm 140 says we're not to keep company with the violent or the wicked. Some one-word definitions of wicked are evil, vicious, harmful, depraved, and immoral. Have any of these words been used to describe your boyfriend or husband? Take a step back and observe him. Does he fit any of the descriptions in the "Breaking it Down" section at the back of this book? If so, I encourage you to leave. The Additional Resources section at the back of the book will give you several places you can turn. Please don't waste another precious minute of your life. I urge you to get help *now*.

Once I decided to file for divorce, I had to figure out how to handle the legal aspect of it. With my smaller paycheck, I didn't feel that I had the money to hire an attorney. I decided to meet with a freelancing paralegal that would be able to assist me in getting the procedure under way. Time would prove that was not the way to go.

I needed to file for a divorce and a restraining order at the same time. The state required that a form be filled out to file for a divorce. It required that I include my employer's name and address, my physical address, and other information that I had worked so hard to keep from my husband. I felt betrayed and unprotected by my new state government. The only consolation was that I was able to use my post office box for my address. (Note: since 9/11/01 a physical address instead of a Post Office Box is required on most legal forms. I was thankful I could use it when I filed for divorce.)

This whole process turned into a fiasco. I still believe to this day that it was due to my husband's ties with the county where he lived and the corruption within that sheriff's department that my husband was not served the papers promptly. He missed at least the first court appearance. If my memory serves me correctly, I believe the papers had to be issued a second time. There were a total of four hearings regarding the restraining order. My husband never showed up for any of them. The judge dismissed it.

One thing that did save my skin was that on both of my jobs, I had used only my post office box as my address. During the divorce proceedings, copies of my paycheck stubs were required. Thankfully, they had that information on them and not my physical address.

Another precaution I knew I was to take was not to use a gas station close to where I lived. Instead, I used gas stations at random. It was one less way I could be traced to a particular neighborhood. That proved to be helpful, as his attorney had access to my checking account—the very one I had worked so hard to keep from my husband.

I had been given some advice to put a portion of my paycheck put into a money order to keep my checking account low. I found out that he had legal rights to half of what was in my checking account. He already had kept money from the children and me that rightfully belonged to us. I was not about to allow him to take any of my hard-earned money.

It wasn't long after my husband received the papers that one of my husband's and my mutual friends came to my new place of employment and demanded that I be called. To this day, I stand amazed at how the Lord protected me. I had the phone right there beside me, yet I never heard it ring. Even though I was sleeping, it should have awakened me. This woman left a very strong message that she wanted me to call. I never did. I loved her and her husband too much to have them get caught in the middle. I chose not to call their phone number. That was difficult, as they were very precious people.

Several things I was informed of during this time sent chills up my spine. First, I found out that my husband said he would fight the divorce to the point of bankruptcy. He was confident he would win because he believed something was wrong with the paperwork. I had no idea what he meant by something being wrong, but I took his threat seriously. I should have known better. Due to his love for money, he never would allow himself to get to the point of bankruptcy.

Then I was told that he wanted our youngest son back with him and that he was looking for our eldest son. I saw this as a desperate move on my husband's part, as he now had no one to control. His entire sense of security had been built around control over us. He was lost without someone to control. How very sad. I did not have to worry about my children, however, as none of them wanted anything more to do with him. They had told me individually that as far as they were concerned, they did not have a father. If for any reason he came up in conversation, they would refer to him by his first name. They've held true to that all these years.

Around this time, I also was told that he was informing people who knew me that I was sick, in the process of getting help, and would return to him. How very wrong he was! That was the last thing I ever would do. My worst nightmares were of being back under his roof. Those made for interesting sessions with the psychologist. I'll talk more about that later.

My son and I soon learned that the cell phone he had sent with me was costing a lot of unnecessary money due to roaming charges. I went on a hunt to see which would be the best company to use for my cell phone provider. When I went in to talk to the company I had chosen, I was waited on by a polite but naïve young man. When it came to the point that he wanted my address to send the bill, I stated my post office box. He politely replied that this company had to have a physical address. I flatly refused and told him I had left an abusive husband and that I would not give out that information. He was surprised to hear that and entered the contact information I gave him. Until I was sure my husband and his attorney had no more access to my checking account, I also paid my cell phone bill with a money order.

Six long, arduous months had gone by since I had left. I was asked to speak at a candlelight vigil during October, National Domestic Violence Awareness Month, and tell my story. I was still very much in a crisis, so my emotions were just under the surface. I made it through that challenge, however, and it turned out to be an indirect way for God to provide for me. The keynote speaker for that evening approached me afterward and offered to pay the cost for me to hire an attorney. I was speechless. This was not an everyday occurrence, and I knew that. God had come through for me once again.

What I found out from my new lawyer surprised me. First of all, he became angry that the judge had dismissed my case requesting an order of protection. He said the judge had no right to do that. He also said that the paperwork I had filled out for the state did not have to have my place of employment or physical address. If I had had an attorney, the office address could have been used. I also could have filed for more of my husband's retirement than I had been advised to do by the paralegal. There also was another minor detail that she had done incorrectly. I realized that I should have saved the money I paid her and begun the process of hiring an attorney.

Not long after this, I found out that my husband had been coming to town weekly to see his lawyer. That didn't do much for any peace of mind I may have had by this time. I was so scared. I was going through all this with few friends at my side and no church to help give me encouragement, roots, or prayer covering. It was truly amazing that I even could get any sleep.

Vivid dreams and nightmares were common. The frequent theme was that I was back with my husband. Each one only added to the terror of my everyday life. It was more than just a difficult time. My counselor told me that dreams are meant to help in the healing process. Yet, as far as I could see, they didn't seem to be advancing me. She asked me if I was considering going back to him. I assured her that was the last thing I would do. It was the sheer terror of that thought that was prompting the dreams.

Even as I look back on all of this, several things stand out in my memory. One is the constant state of fear, and another is how I cried out to the Lord for help like never before. I also saw God with new eyes. I saw vividly how He was my Provider, Protector, Refuge, Shelter, Strength, Wisdom, Peace, and my very Rock. I will forever be a different woman, as I have seen the reality of who He is through the toughest time in my life. No one can take that

DIRECTIONS

knowledge or experience away from me. Beyond a shadow of a doubt, I *know* He is real and is my true Source for every need I have. During one session with my psychologist, I told her about a recent dream I'd had. I told her that in my dream I stood up to my husband and told him the truth instead of just cowering. I said I never would have reacted that way when I was with him in a situation like that. She said dreams are indicators of progress in your healing. As time has gone on, I've come to believe that to be true. Through the years, I have become more than just bold as I've confronted him in my dreams. Hopefully, there will come a day when I no longer have him occupying my hours of sleep. I am grateful the nightmares are seldom now.

One day my son had someone show up at one of his jobs. The strange questions the man asked raised our suspicions. As my son relayed what had happened, we both became concerned that it could have been a private investigator. I alerted my co-workers so they wouldn't give out any information in case he came to my place of employment.

My mom asked me for my feedback one

day as I talked with her. My husband had continued to give them gifts on holidays and birthdays, and she was uncomfortable with this. She wanted to know if she should contact him to say they did not want any more presents and to tell him to stop coming to see her and my stepfather. I was very supportive of her drawing healthy boundaries with him. She decided to send him a letter. When he received it, he called her. He told my mom that he hadn't gone out and bought the gifts he'd given them, but that he had them on hand. Not only was this totally unlike him to have gifts ahead of time, but he had told our daughter he had bought the gifts for my mom and stepfather.

    The more this divorce drama went on, the more of a mess it turned out to be. Each fresh piece of news meant more garbage to sludge through. I was so very weary of it all. Yet I would go through it again to have the freedom I have today. My life is so opposite to what I had when I was under my husband's control. Because I got away from his clutches, I now am healthier emotionally, physically, and spiritually than I ever have been in my life. One reason I believe this is true is that I was determined to get through the divorce without having any resentment or bitterness when it was all over. I had seen too many people in my life who still were bitter about things that happened years ago. I saw how it even affected their physical health. I was resolute that I would come out of it, in every respect, better than I was going in. I had read that unforgiveness breeds instability. If there was anything I did not need, it was more instability. I plowed through each difficult time, trying to process each piece of information with that goal in mind. It was a fight, but I am so glad I went at it with such determination, as I have come out of it the winner.

My daughter and I'd had sporadic communication from the time I left. Now she was contacting me more often. Her father would not leave her alone. He had begun to come to her place frequently. During those visits, she began to see a change in him that frightened her. It culminated when, following a previous incident that left her very uncomfortable with him, he knocked on her door five times in one day. Then a police car was seen outside her apartment repeatedly. And

she also had seen a black truck outside her window over and over again. She was getting rattled. The abusive boyfriend she just had broken up with was stalking her as well. What she needed more than anything was to get away. Soon, she and my grandson were able to come to visit me for three days. And within a month, she moved just a few doors down from me. It was so good to have
two of my three children and my grandson with me.

It was about this time that I began to realize that I was not receiving all my mail that should have been forwarded from the town I'd fled from. It was then that I found out what I should have done at the time I left: I needed to write the Postmaster and request that all my mail be routed to my new address. Even though it was months after I'd fled, time had been wasted, and my husband very possibly was sent a change of address by the Post Office (giving him my new location), I sent a letter anyway. In it, I stated that even though I had put in a change of address form, not all of my mail was arriving at my new address. I also requested that my husband not be notified of this request

DIRECTIONS

either by computer-generated notification or through the Postmaster's office. My son and daughter requested the same service. All three letters were mailed together.

One day, as I was about to leave to run errands, my daughter called me and asked where I was. I told her I was still at home. She had an unusually serious tone to her voice as she told me not to go anywhere today. My husband just had been spotted in town. I didn't have to be told twice. I laid low.

Before I arrived at work that night, my supervisor had received several odd calls. This had gone on for five hours, at the same time each hour, and then stopped when I showed up at work. Then that night, the strangest thing happened. Each time I walked by the window or front door, the phone in the adjoining office rang. It rarely ever rang throughout the night. This went on for hours. I intentionally walked by in full view, even when I didn't need to, just to see if that triggered it. It always did. This is the only time it ever happened in the two years I was there. I continued to look out the window by the desk, but I couldn't see anyone. I wasn't timidly looking either. I was giving intimidating looks. Then, about the time my son would have gotten off work, it stopped.

Although I have no proof, I believe that my husband watched me from a nearby parking garage that night and then followed our son home from work. It would have been easy for him to do, as our son still had the unique car he had owned when he still lived with my husband.

I found out about two weeks later that my husband had talked to the manager of our apartment complex about the same time he had been spotted in town. When I brought in a picture of him, her countenance changed. She was horrified to find out that was my husband and said he had scared her. He had sat down in a very strategic location in the lobby, where he could see all the traffic coming and going from the complex. He also asked several ridiculous questions just to make conversation. Some of the things he asked her were: "What is the largest vehicle you have here on the property?" "What kinds of cars do the tenants drive?" Although it was posted on the front door of the office that a driver's license was required before an apartment could be seen, he refused to show

DIRECTIONS

her any form of identification, saying, "I am not going to be seeing an apartment, so I don't have to show you anything." He had stayed until he was ready to leave.

When I found out about all this, I began my investigation. I slept in split shifts to carry this out. I would come home, sleep for about four hours, go to other area apartment complexes to see if he had been there seeking information on me, and then come home and sleep for another four hours before going to work. It was exhausting, but for my own sanity, I needed to know the truth. This whole process took about two weeks. During that entire time, the only person I found who recognized his picture was someone who had seen him at a local gas station. No one else had seen him or been asked questions by him. My husband felt very confident that he had found where we lived. It confirmed my theory that my husband probably had followed my son home from work.

In light of that, I made a second round of visits to the local law enforcement. This time, the volunteer from the first shelter went with me. Again, I spoke directly with the sheriff, my new police chief, and the Assistant Chief of Police in the neighboring city. Of course, no one admitted that they had been contacted by him. I knew that I would need to be more vigilant if that was even possible.

During the two years that I had the job on the graveyard shift, I placed two handwritten signs outside my door each morning when I came home from work that asked people to leave a message and not knock, as I was sleeping. I found that I had to have more than one, as one sign didn't seem to get the message across. Having two signs helped to ensure that I would get a full day's sleep in. Several times, these signs came up missing. I instantly suspected my husband. But I knew that it also could have been the kids on the property just having fun. So I made another sign, glued it to a large magnet, and placed it toward the top of my door, out of reach of the kids. After a while, it disappeared. I was more than suspicious this time.

Next, I tried having a friend write the two signs for me. They stayed for quite a while. Then one day after I woke up, I went to take the signs down. I found both perfectly stacked

DIRECTIONS

against the wall, placed halfway between my apartment and the next. Oddly enough, the ones in my handwriting never reappeared. The signs I found had been written by the shelter volunteer. That perfectly fit what I knew my husband would do—save something written by my own hand. For all I know, he may have been planning to use it in court against me somehow. Possibly he was going to keep it as a private trophy for himself to show that he'd found me. Whatever the reason, I felt strongly that my husband had done that intentionally to send me a message. He was a neat nick, so the placement as well as the condition of being neatly stacked fit the way he operated. At best, it was extremely eerie. My alertness to my surroundings heightened even more.

Now that I was fairly certain that my husband knew where we lived, I became even more careful of how I handled my trash. I found out when trash pickup was, and I did not put the trash in the dumpster until the last possible minute. I know to some people it sounded absurd, but I did not put it past him to take what he thought was my bag of trash and then sift through it later. I began to be even more careful to shred anything that he did not need to read. I no longer felt comfortable disposing of any items at work that I did not want him to get his hands on. Also, knowing how well he followed someone, I would not even put anything in the trash container on my way into the grocery store, as he might be in the parking lot observing me and come and retrieve what I had put in. It seemed ridiculous to those who never had seen that side of him, but our children and I knew what he was like. I truly could not be too careful.

After one incident nine months after I'd left my husband, I recounted to my psychologist the latest bizarre behavior he was exhibiting. She said that he was "not balanced," "getting unstable," and had an "unnatural attachment to the marriage." How much more alert could I possibly be to his next move? She told me in another session that it was up to me to choose what would disrupt my life and asked if I was going to allow that. I really appreciated her honesty and wisdom. I benefited greatly from this precious woman.

My psychologist told me in yet another session that I can't let darkness and forebodings have the upper hand. She said I was making my husband into a giant and that what I needed to remember was that God is the giant killer. I knew I needed to hear that. What I could not seem to get past was the possibility of what could happen. That truly was so overwhelming. I struggled between her statement and the truth of what I knew my husband was and the possibilities of just what he was capable of. Then the Lord gave me Exodus 14:13–14, which says,

"...do not be afraid. Stand firm and you will see the deliverance the Lord will bring you today... The Lord will fight for you; you need only to be still" (Today's NIV).

I knew God was telling me to not fear, but I remained terrified. Almost daily He would lead me to a portion of Scripture that I needed. Yet I could not seem to get my eyes off the frightening circumstances and onto His promises. Fear can destroy hope. I was living proof of that. Fear was sucking the hope right out from under me.

If only I had listened better to God.

FREE TO SOAR

FREEDOM!

...I will call on God, and the Lord will rescue me. Morning, noon, and night I cry out in my distress, and the Lord hears my voice. He ransoms me and keeps me safe from the battle waged against me... (Psalm 55:16-18 NLT)

Several months after my daughter and grandson moved to my new town, she filed for an order of protection from her father. She wanted to protect her son as well as herself since we knew my husband had been in town. A court date was set, and he was summoned for the court appearance. Although he never had shown up for any of my court appearances, I knew he would show up for hers.

When it came time for her court appearance, just as I predicted, he came. Along with my daughter and youngest son, there were two friends plus the court advocate from the shelter with us for support. My husband pulled his "poor me" body language and shuffled over to where we were seated outside the courtroom. He sarcastically wagged his head and said, "Hello." We all ignored him as though he wasn't there. When he walked over to us, we were laughing over something that had been said among us. He shuffled on into the courtroom. No sooner had he rounded the corner, than I began to tremble. I was terrified to be that close to him.

In just a few short minutes, it was time for the court to convene. I couldn't stop shaking. The tension in that courtroom was thick. The entire room was filled with other people who also were seeking an order of protection. It seemed to take forever to hear each case. We were not at the beginning of the docket.

Finally, my daughter's name was called. Her father took his place at the table opposite her. He had his briefcase, filled with documentation, I was sure. He had so much experience appearing before a judge on his job. I knew beyond a shadow of a doubt that he was fully prepared to defend his case. Fortunately, the judge cut to the chase. It was obvious by his tone he was hesitant to award her any protection from her father. We never had pressed charges against him, nor were there any police records against him. But with his excellent standings with four different law enforcement agencies where he still lived, we both had known it would have been pointless. Both he and his brother could talk their way out of anything. With no evidence before him, the judge had no grounds to award her legal protection.

Then my daughter spoke up and informed the judge that her father recently had been seen in town and that we had reason to believe he was looking for us. Immediately, my husband's body language completely changed. His shoulders slumped. He looked like a deflated balloon. He had no idea we'd known he was in town. The judge changed his tune and awarded her protection for one year. What relief!

We couldn't get out of that courtroom fast enough. Even then, we divided up into several cars, all fully aware that my husband easily could follow any one of us. We strategically went in different directions to prevent leading him to where we lived. My adrenaline was running high. It took another hour or two after I arrived home for my trembling to stop.

The next month, my youngest son moved back to the town where his father lived so he could play his last eligible season of baseball. He knew he might receive a college scholarship while he was there. If not, he planned to join the military. I was afraid for him, as our nation was in a war, but I also was terrified without my son near me to protect me from his father. The divorce was not yet final, and I knew my husband would need to be in town for that.

My immediate future was still so uncertain and so very scary for me. Just before my son's leaving, I'd had to go to see a doctor for a simple thing, but I broke down due to the stress. I wrote in my journal, "I don't feel I can take much more." I truly had no idea if I indeed could take any more. Although I didn't know it, I was about halfway through this long, dark journey. There was a light at the end of the tunnel, but I hadn't rounded the corner to see it yet.

Not long after my son left, I had a vivid nightmare that I still recall. In my dream, my husband walked through my apartment patio door into the living room. I called for my son more than once to come from the bedroom, yet he never came out. I was terrified. I woke up before the dream ended, but I knew as my husband walked closer and closer to me that he was at the very least going to harm me. I felt unprotected. Life was so very difficult. I was afraid of what lay ahead for me. I did my best just to get on with my life.

I now slept in the twin bed my son had occupied. This felt safe and secure to me, much as the couch had, as there was no room for two people. It also felt much safer to be in a bedroom where I could close the door. Yet I was not sleeping well. I only averaged between four to six hours per night. Also, my daughter was adding drama on almost a daily basis. Life was not good then. A friend kept close tabs on me.

As I felt comfortable talking to people I had met some would say not to worry, because he wasn't going to hurt me. However, each time I heard someone say that, it became more and more frustrating. No one knew the future. No one could tell me with certainty what my husband would or would not do. Hearing one person's opinion only sent my mind into another tailspin of terrifying thoughts of what he was capable of and what he might do. It negated all the comforting words I heard. It didn't take much to send my mind into a tornadic whirl of what might happen to me.

One day as I was in my little kitchen, I had a most unusual flashback. It was as though I was coming in the back door of the house where we used to live and getting ready to walk into the kitchen there. It was all so vivid. Yet this flashback was different than the brief ones I commonly had throughout the day. I could feel my hopelessness and the intense oppression that was in the house whenever my husband was at home. Just as quickly as it had come, it left. I was now once again back in my cozy, little apartment that I loved. What had just happened?

A few days later, I told a friend about my flashback. I was surprised that I had to stifle back sobs as I recounted it to her. Then at my next appointment with my psychologist, I described it to her. The emotions were there again. Even the very memory of that flashback was so very vivid. She shared with me that it was a sign that I was in the healing process. That was such a relief to know. It was just one more reason for me to be grateful that I had her walking me through this difficult time and opening my understanding to things such as this. Otherwise, I would have wondered if I was losing it. As the years have gone on, the small flashbacks don't come nearly as often. I've never had a vivid one like that again.

My husband now had the idea that I was not coming back. He communicated through our attorneys that he had things of mine that I could pick up. There was no way I was going to come face-to-face with him, so I contacted two very dear friends that lived in the same city where he was. They were more than willing to pick up the items he had deemed I could have. I then called my mom and stepdad to see if these two friends could deliver my things to their house so I could come and pick them up as soon as I was able to get there. They agreed to this arrangement.

After my friends picked up my things, they confirmed the strange emotional and spiritual climate that I had lived in. One of my friends said she didn't know how I'd lived under that. That was such a comfort to hear, as my husband almost had convinced me that I was crazy before I left.

When I made the trip to my mom's house to pick up my things, I was so terrified to be back in town. I had no idea if I would see my husband or some of his friends. As I got closer to town, I put on a cap, sunglasses, and a hooded jacket in an attempt to disguise myself. I also was very aware that he possibly was keeping an eye on my mom's house, so when I arrived, I parked so the out-of-state license plates were not visible from the road.

It turned out that there were more things than I was able to pack into my little car, so I had to sort through everything. Some of the items I threw away, but then I later caught my mom and stepdad going through my bag of trash. I grew more cautious of what I got rid of. A few items I even took back with me to throw them away at my apartment.

I didn't stay overnight but completed the round trip in one day. It was nerve-wracking enough to be in the same town as my husband; I did not want to stay any longer than I had to.

It now was getting closer to the time for our divorce. It seemed I was not just on the edge of my seat, but I was poised with muscles tensed, ready to spring up at a moment's notice. I had no idea what to expect. Thankfully, my psychologist helped to prepare me for what might lie ahead. She also willingly agreed to testify in court on my behalf. But just before we were to go to court, a new law was passed that stated that if she testified, *all* the records of our sessions would be open for my husband's attorney to subpoena. It was an incredibly tough decision, but I ultimately decided not to have her testify.

God spoke to me so many times through the scriptures or books I read. One thing I read during that time said, "The battle is God's, and He always wins." [5]

There was a seemingly constant flood of reassuring messages God kept sending me, yet I could not get a handle on that hope due to the fear that gripped me.

One book that I read during this time was by Stormie Omartian. It was entitled *Just Enough Light for the Step I'm On*. In it, I learned that God perfects our hearts when we suffer. He uses that and makes us humble and compassionate, two traits we must have to be successful in what He has for us to do. We need to stand strong through the fire, and we'll be purified, molded, humbled, and made ready for what He has for us. This was not only encouraging to me, but also it helped me to see something that I'm not sure I would have otherwise seen—a future. I had been living in survival mode for so long, and I couldn't see much more than the immediate present. To even think of looking ahead gave me a sense of hope. *Single Again and Secure in God's Love* by Jim Smoke was another book that inspired me to continue and look beyond the current crisis I was in.

During this time, I was not the only one dealing with a crisis. My daughter had her own issues to deal with. I already had dealt with a lot of drama related to my daughter, but I was unprepared for what she threw at me next. She wanted to know if I would be willing to adopt my grandson in a few months. Little did I know that by this point in time, she had reconnected with her former boyfriend, who had been abusive both to her and my grandson. Before this, he had no idea where she was, so I knew that she had to have been the one who had initiated contact. She was. I was furious. Numerous people had worked so hard to get her moved to a safe place. Now their very safety was in jeopardy. I made sure she realized that because he was abusive, my safety was now at risk, too.

It didn't sink in. In less than two weeks, he came and moved my daughter and grandson out in the middle of the night. The next day, I found my possessions that had been at her place neatly stacked on my patio. It was a wonder they hadn't all been stolen while I was at work. I knew that her boyfriend had been the one who had climbed over the railing and put them there, as my daughter wasn't physically capable of that. Now I had him to be concerned about, too. They returned to the city they'd grown up in and married. My heart was broken. I was living with the reality of the national statistics that a victim will return to his or her abuser six to eight times before leaving the abuser for good. It was one thing for her to decide to go back to a known abuser, but her choice to put my grandson in harm's way was almost more than I could take.

My youngest son returned right before

the divorce hearing; his brother was not able to get away from work. Their support was invaluable and still is. It felt so much safer to have at least one of my sons with me. They are very protective of me and would not let their father come near me. Both of them have been pillars of strength through every ordeal. I am so very grateful for my two very strong young men.

A very interesting twist came about on the day of the divorce hearing. I received a call from my lawyer's office. They said that my husband wanted to settle out of court. I was surprised. I wondered what had happened to his willingness to fight to the point of bankruptcy. Although I was very afraid to be in the same courtroom with him again, I felt I was as prepared for the ordeal as I possibly could be. Still, this turn of events was welcome.

Through a series of phone calls, my husband and I came to an agreement. In less than a month, I was a free woman. I did not look at it as free in the sense of being able to get married again but as free from abuse of every kind, free from the legal ties to him, free from any debt he could impose on me, free from his

FREEDOM!

oppressive spiritual nature, and free from his hold on me. There was such a wonderful release. I found it to be truly indescribable. I felt more at liberty than I ever had before.

FREE TO SOAR

RENOVATED

...God takes the side of victims. Do you think you can mess with the dreams of the poor? You can't, for God makes their dreams come true. (Psalm 14:5-6 MSG)

Until I felt this new freedom and release, I didn't realize what a dangerous place I had been in. My existence before the finalization of the divorce had been moment by moment. I had lived on sheer adrenaline, going from one crisis to the next. Although I still needed to be vigilant about my surroundings, it was not nearly as critical. I was emotionally exhausted. Physically, I had no energy. I went to work and did my job, but nothing more. I felt numb on the inside.

Because I was not in constant crisis mode anymore, I no longer was desperate for what had been my source of strength—Jesus and the Bible. I found excuses not to pick up my Bible and read it each day. I rarely talked to God for wisdom, strength, or help. Just as not working out daily in the gym will cause you to lose strength, so will pulling away from the true Source of strength. Spiritually, I slowly began to sink. Little did I know that I was repeating my father's behavior.

My youngest son left for boot camp to join the Marine Corps just six months after the divorce was finalized. I knew he desired to be on the front lines of the war. My older son was depressed and going through his own difficulties. At the same time, I could feel I was slowly headed to the same place. How could I help him when I was slipping away myself? I began to wonder just how much more these drooping shoulders of mine could handle. I felt so very overwhelmed. I did my best to move forward one step at a time. I so desperately wanted and needed to begin my life over again.

As I started to have more time to devote to ordinary life, I finally began to catch up on my emails. I had hundreds to go through. I began to think about possibly joining one of the internet social networking sites. I eventually made the huge step and joined. I never put any pictures of myself on it, even though it was set up with the most private settings. Then both of my sons notified me that my ex-husband had tried to contact them by leaving them messages on their sites. I immediately shut mine down.

There was no way I was going to take that chance. Recently, my oldest son told me that it's still not safe for me to have my own site. That's all right for now. My life is moving forward. I refuse to allow something that trivial to affect my attitude.

Once the divorce was final, it felt as though a huge weight had been lifted from my shoulders. I finally could go forward with my life. Yet, honestly, I had no idea how to do that. I still felt numb. Aspects of my life were so very heavy, so dark, and oppressive. At times, I even felt as though I was dying deep within. I knew I had hope and a purpose for my life or I wouldn't have gotten away from my husband safely. Yet so much had crashed down on me. I just didn't feel as though I could stand up and go on. What I should have done was start using my spare time to indulge myself with the activities that make me happy, pampering myself with whatever helps me to relax should have been on the agenda. Unfortunately, that wasn't what I did. Although I continued with my job and the basic routine of life, I had lost my determination to plow through the difficulties. I began to wither away on the inside. I pulled away from the very One who had guided me, protected me, and provided for my every need. I began to lean on people.

During that time one friend told me she was amazed that I hadn't had a nervous breakdown. Looking back, I am, too.

Not once, but twice I almost completely walked away from the Lord. Yet He was gently and lovingly calling me back. After at least six months, I decided to turn my life around. It was like a big ship doing a 180-degree turn. Although living my life for God was my new destination, it took quite a while before He was the focus of my new scenery and my old habits were behind me. It has been a long journey for me to get that slow boat back to where it was before it headed in the wrong direction. I now wear a ring as a sign of my commitment to Him. It signifies that I will not leave Him again. I may get weak in the knees, but I will not turn and walk away. The awesome part of this journey is that the closer I choose to get to Him, the more joy I have. He is once again my Source of wisdom and direction. He is also my best friend.

RENOVATED

As I think back on all the overwhelming things I went through while trying to get free from my abusive husband, I see one silver lining to it all: I learned so much, and those things never can be taken from me. As I pressed through the dark times of life, there was a wonderful, unexpected reward on the other side. The types of valuable lessons I learned never can be obtained in the good times of life. They are learned as we plow ahead through the hard times and growth takes place deep within us. When we keep pressing on through our struggles, we become more rock solid on the other side of them. One of my friends whom I have known for over thirty years told me, "I've seen chunks just fall off you through all this; you're so completely different than you were before." She could see my growth. Let me encourage you. If you are going through difficult times, accept where you are as a jumping-off point for your future. Thankfully, things won't always stay this way if you continue to move forward.

There is still healing that needs to take place in me. For example, I often pull away if I am unexpectedly touched from behind. When I was in a session with the psychologist, I asked her why. She told me it is due to the trauma I'd experienced. She advised me to ask trusted friends to come up behind me and touch me to help me relearn that I'm safe.

Another example is when I am verbally or emotionally abused at work, it can throw me off for days. If it's someone I know and at one time trusted, it can be weeks before I snap out of it and back into the healthy flow of life. God has done an incredible job of healing inside of me, but I'm far from perfect.

Even though I live in a remote area, I still use caution when it comes to cars following me when I come home at night. Recently, I had an untagged car in front of me as I headed home. I went into alert mode right away. I have preparations in place that at times like that I rehearse and am fully prepared for. First of all, I purposely do not go directly home. Instead, I drive around the area to watch and see where the other vehicle goes. If it ever was apparent that I indeed was being followed, I would call certain trusted friends who have made themselves available twenty-four hours a day. Then I would drive to the police department, remain in my locked car, and lay on the horn until help arrived at my window. Thankfully, I've never had to implement the last two steps of that plan.

Once I began to have a little breathing room with my time, I began asking the Lord what I could do to repay the three shelters that helped me start a new life. I've found some ways to give back through volunteering. One thing I do is collect donations and deliver them to the shelter so the women and children have needed clothing and supplies for their new homes. I was amazed when I stayed there at how many basic items were needed. The thing that surprised me the most is how fast used linens disappeared from the shelves and never returned, especially washcloths, towels, dishcloths, and dish towels. I then realized that these women were thinking ahead about what they would need when they got out on their own. Truly, it's so rewarding to me to deliver essentials for the new lives of these courageous women who have taken the risk of leaving their abusers. I long to give them hope for what's ahead in life if they just will continue to move forward, even if it's just one slow step at a time.

That's one reason I've written this book. My heart longs to be able to put a copy into the hands of each woman as she enters a domestic violence shelter, or as I prefer to call it now: a safe house. I want these women to know that there's a whole world of possibilities out there beyond the secluded life they've been forced to exist in.

When I was going through all those gloomy, black days of my life, I felt as though they never would end. My life felt so hopeless. I didn't want to live a life full of intense struggles, suffocating stress levels, and a constant string of crises. I didn't even realize it, but through the time spent talking to my counselor, freely releasing the tears, writing out my feelings, and the passage of time, a healing transformation was taking place in me. It was as though I finally began to awaken after the months I had lived in the dark shadows of life. I found that I began to smile. Then I would find myself laughing. The heaviness of my intense grieving was gone. The intensity of one mind-boggling crisis after another had been like carrying a backpack loaded with rocks. Now the backpack was unloaded. It felt so good! I truly had forgotten how to act without the constant presence of my familiar anguish. It was foreign to have it gone. I suddenly discovered that I was enjoying my life! It felt so strange that I had to step back and figure out what was going on inside of me. I struggled with some guilt over it. I don't anymore, though.

As unusual as it sounds, I truly did have to learn how to enjoy life. Just as a baby begins to take one shaky step at a time, I've had to discover how to walk through life one stride at a time. Now I enjoy my new life *immensely*. I love the freedom I have! I relish in the little things life brings, like beautiful flowers, sunsets reflected on the water, watching the moon come up, seeing the wildlife around me, and the birds cavorting right on my balcony. I laugh a lot these days, too. My dark, heavy past is just that: the past. It used to be that my past controlled my present and my future. Now my future sets the direction and tone of my life. I feel like a bird set free from its cage; I am no longer bound by my past. I try to live in the present. Even when I get into living for the future, I get out of balance. I just try to enjoy the moment.

I still have struggles, heartache, and trials within my relationships. My life is not perfect. I do not have it all together. Life is not completely figured out in my head. Yet I wouldn't trade what I have for what I came out of. I am free from my harassing, abusive, conniving, manipulative, unstable ex-husband. Now I'm free to apply for any job I want. I can live anywhere I choose. Supper does not have to be ready at a precise time. No longer do I need to tremble in fear when I go to the store No longer am I concerned that I will spend more than what he allotted. Now if I need something shredded, I don't need to take it to the shelter where I stayed; I just use my shredder. I feel so free not to have to worry about what I put in the trash because of the fear that he will go through it and gain valuable information about me. Now it simply goes into the dumpster. After I left him, I had to be so careful about what pay phone and gas station I used. Now I use my cell phone and one gas station. Before the divorce, I paid my rent, utilities, and cell phone with money orders since I knew his attorney would have access to my checking account information. Now I either write a check or pay online. These are minor examples, yet in so many aspects, my life is different. I am so very grateful.

In the last few years, I went through an even more intense time of inner healing. I met periodically with a dear friend for about two years. During that time, we went even deeper into my past. I was able to forgive people who had harmed me emotionally. Looking deep inside myself, I faced up to my own mistakes and asked forgiveness from God and others. This truly has brought me to a place I've never been before. So much of what weighed me down is gone. There is a new level of freedom that is unlike anything I've ever known.

I went on my first date in over thirty years. That was a new chapter in my life for sure. My daily pattern is that of volunteering, collecting donations for the women's shelters, having a purpose in my job, sharing laughter with my co-workers, performing household duties, staying in touch with friends, reading, and sleeping peacefully. I honestly don't think it could be any more opposite from what it was.

Freedom and an abundance of possibilities exist for any victim out there, whether it's you or someone you know. It is *always* achievable to escape an abuser and have a brand-new life that is free from violence and neglect. Please get help for yourself or a friend you know who is in a bad situation. Time is too precious to waste. Make a change for the better, and get started now.

If you are the victim or think you might be, please learn from my story that you *can* get free. There is a whole world outside the little, suffocating one you're in right now. I cannot stress it enough: get out *now*, while you're still able to. A fantastic place to start is calling the *National Coalition Against Domestic Violence Hotline, at 1-800-799-7233*. Even though the thought of leaving is terrifying, do it afraid. You have nothing to lose and everything to gain. Another resource is dialing 211. Just as 911 is a siren call, 211 will help put you in touch with organizations that are ready and waiting to help you. You'll be amazed at all that is available to assist you as you strive to begin your life all over again. Look in the Resources section at the back of this book for more information as to what they offer.

Before I close, I want to make it clear that this book is not meant to be an exposé of my ex-husband. If I had wanted to do that, I would have used his name. It also is not meant to be a pity party for my "poor, pitiful life." That's why I have not used names as I've written this. I've poured out my story before you to help get true victims away from their abusers and into brand new lives of freedom.

Are you being abused on an occasional or daily basis? Or are you abusing anyone around you? Answering this question requires that you take a good, hard look at yourself. Has the way you treat your spouse, children, or pets been labeled as abusive? If you've answered "yes" to any of these questions, please get help right now.

FREE TO SOAR

EPILOGUE

If the Lord had not been on our side—let Israel now say—if the Lord had not been on our side when people rose up against us, they would have swallowed us alive because of their burning anger against us. The waters would have engulfed us; a torrent would have overwhelmed us.

Yes, the raging waters of their fury would have overwhelmed our very lives. Blessed be the Lord, who did not let their teeth tear us apart! We escaped like a bird from a hunter's trap. The trap is broken, and we are free! Our help is from the Lord, Who made the heavens and the earth. (Psalm 124 NLT)

As of the writing of this book, I have had no contact with my daughter for years. Since the first edition of this book was published, I was told that my daughter had a baby girl. I've never met her. I look forward to getting to know her in the future. My oldest grandson and I missed out on twelve years of his life, but we are now reconnected. Both he and his sister suffer the emotional effects of my daughter's upbringing.

FREE TO SOAR

My mom died at the age of 92. I believed it would have been detrimental to her if she had known, so I never told her that it existed. She was always so concerned about what others thought if they knew the truth. Part of this is due to the generation she grew up in. Society did not accept people opening up and discussing sensitive issues. I also believe my mom is ashamed and feels guilty about what my biological father did. The shame was his. He was the sick one who needed help. Since Mom did feel guilty about what my dad did, I truly believe that only God knows if she was guilty of not stepping in on our behalf. And even if she is, I don't hold that against her at all. My father was an unpredictable angry man. She was afraid of him, and she had good reason to be.

I lost contact with my father before I got married, for which I am grateful. Ever since I stopped hearing from him, each day has been blissfully more peaceful than the previous one. I never have heard of a psychological diagnosis for him, but I can assure you that he desperately needed help. Mom found out several years ago that Dad had died, and my brother died just a few months later. That was a huge relief to

EPILOGUE

Mom, my sister, and I. We all were afraid Dad would find us and cause trouble. Before he died, he had a voodoo doll of each of us. That's quite a far cry from a Protestant pastor who at one time loved Jesus.

My brother reconnected with our father and became an extremely angry man like Dad.

My sons are my heroes. Despite all they endured as they grew up, they both chose to join the military. I swell with pride each time I think of them. Enlisting in a career where they would be ordered around mercilessly as they were for eighteen years was the last thing I would have anticipated them wanting to do.

I had no contact with my stepfather in the last years of his life. There are only four from his family that I care to have interaction with. Continuing to have unhealthy communication takes its toll on the people involved. I want to be as healthy as possible, so I choose not to allow them to drag me down.

The only friendship that my husband was successful in cutting off is now restored. Sandy, it is awesome to have you back in my life!

I now have moved twenty-eight times. Needless to say, I'm tired of moving. Only God knows how many more times I'll need to move before I make my final move to His home in heaven. It sure makes me grateful for having been in one location for almost four years. I thank the Lord all the time for this peaceful place.

So, is my life free from hurt? No. Am I free from abuse? Yes! And I'm becoming freer as I continue to work on getting healthier emotionally. This is intentional behavior.

If you're hurting, I want to encourage you that relief eventually does come. Persevere. It's worth it. When adequate time, medicine, and attention are given to a wound, it eventually does heal. Neglect of a wound only intensifies the damage. Infection can set in, which, if left untreated, could lead to death. Are there scars left from my hurts? Yes. That's what happens when a deep wound heals. The scar is merely a reminder of what happened. I've had enough hurts in my life; I don't want any more. I chose a long time ago to work through the pain with the intent of getting to the place of healing.

EPILOGUE

No matter where you are in the struggles of life, I want to let you know that it's not necessarily going to remain that way. Honestly, life isn't so much about what happens to us as it is about how we deal with it. I like to use word pictures. So, we're going to use the analogy of a tunnel. If you find yourself in a tunnel, choose to dig your way out. Please don't just sit down and give up. You don't want to die in a dark, mucky place like that. Sit down and take a rest; that's fine. You need to rest because this work is *hard*. But then get up and start digging and plowing through again. It's worth it. There eventually will be light at the other end of the tunnel. Be sure you're using the right tools: counseling, as well as strong friends who will continue to stand by you. It will be very painful if you're trying to get through by yourself, which can be equated to digging with your bare hands. You run the risk of further injury, not to mention that it definitely will take longer.

My most important tool during my process of digging out was Jesus. He already knew what was on the other side of that dirt wall before I began to dig. He guided me through, around the large rocks that could have injured me or slowed me down. If you're wondering why the God of the universe didn't do the work for me, He could have. He's strong enough. However, He gives us the freedom to choose. I needed to choose to escape my abusive ex-husband. Then I chose to get help to become emotionally healthy. I chose to plow through the divorce and come out on the other side of it without bitterness. And to help you get out of your situation, I chose to sit down and relive my pain as I wrote this book.

If I didn't think you could be released from the junk you've found yourself in, I never would have gone through the arduous task of typing out the most painful time in my life for the whole world to read. It would be pointless. It merely would be another book on the shelf. What's the point of that? No, I have a deep, burning desire to offer you a helping hand and an encouraging word to keep on. Freedom *is* possible. Make good use of the people out there who are just waiting to assist you.

There are so many resources out there to be used, and I want to point you to the most important one. I have had some incredible friends in my life, but none like this one. My

EPILOGUE

best friend has nudged me on the right course when I asked Him for help, provided for me financially when I saw no way out, calmed me down when I wouldn't hush up long enough to listen, comforted me when sobs threatened to tear my insides apart, protected me when I asked for His help and infused His strength in me when I needed it. His name is Jesus.

Now before you shut this book and slam it down, just listen to me. Who is allowed on the witness stand in a courtroom? Someone the attorney knows has been an eyewitness to at least a portion of the case being presented. I am sitting on the witness stand. I saw over and over how Jesus directed me when I was being pulled in several directions. He gave me strength when I just couldn't go on any longer. He always made sure I had what I needed, whether it was money to pay the bills, food to eat, or some other necessity. He covered me with His peace when I should have been a nervous wreck. Most times, I threw off His blanket of peace and chose to stay in my nervous, miserable state. Again, that was my choice. He always has been there when I've cried until I thought my heart would break into pieces. I have found myself in some potentially dangerous situations. Each time, He brought me out safely. Not only am I fully convinced that He does exist, but I also know that He has taken care of me throughout my entire life.

Now, before you even go there, let me say that I don't think I'm anybody special. I just happen to know that He loves you just as much as He loves me. I know He would love to be there for you, to help you just like He's always done for me. But there's one thing you need to know about Him: He's a true gentleman. He won't go where He's not welcome. He won't barge into your house, even if you hold the door wide open. You need to ask Him to come inside. Even then, He won't go into any room unless he's invited. Once He's in a room, He won't even sit down unless you ask Him to. You have to make the first move. If you could open the front door of your life, you'd find Him standing there. As you're reading this, it's like the doorbell ringing. If you want Him in, just ask Him. Use your own words. I heard one young man ask God if he could jump on His train. Tell Jesus you want Him to drive the train, or run every room of your house. Just express it in a

EPILOGUE

way that makes sense to you. He will be able to understand you. Believe me when I say that He's more than ready to help you. Here's an example of what you can say if you want to: "Jesus, I've made a mess of things. I've done a lot of things wrong in my life. I'm sorry. Please forgive me. I want You in my life. I want You to run my life for me, please. I'm Yours now. Thank You."

Next, tell somebody what you've just done. Call 1-800-NEED-HIM if you don't know who to tell. Get an easy-to-read Bible and start in the book of John. Then you find a church that will teach you from the Bible what this new relationship is all about. All this can transform your life, but the choice is yours. After the divorce, I wrote in my journal: I'm free!!!!!!!!!!!!!!!!!!!!!!!!!!!!!! This marks the beginning of a new life. Thank You, Jesus! I know it won't be final until thirty days after the judge signs off, but having seen what my husband signed –Wow! — admitting the marriage was irretrievably broken when all along he had been pressing hard for reconciliation. Oh, God, thank You for freedom from him! Thank You that those ties are finally severed! Now that they are severed legally, may they please be severed spiritually. May total healing come to my entire body now that he is no longer my spiritual head (leader). Please, may I have a renewed mind and no longer have echoes of his comments running through my brain. I pray that my battered spirit, which I believe would have eventually become broken, be fully mended and restored. Please heal me up on the inside so that I can have strong, solid friendships.

My counselor prayed with me in a session not too long after I found out the divorce was final. I prayed for a total severing of ties to my ex-husband— spiritually, emotionally, sexually, and in every other way. I wanted a full recovery. I longed to be as whole emotionally as I possibly could be. A few years later, I had a friend send me a prayer written by Dr. Gary Wood[6]. If you're ready to have the garbage of your abusive life, be ancient history, feel free to use this as a pattern: Father, I come to You in the Name of Jesus and I ask You to send angels to gather and restore my soul to its rightful place in me with the full power and authority of Jesus Christ. I ask You to send angels to unearth and break all earthen vessels, bonds, bands, and bindings that have been put on my soul (my mind, will, and emotions), willingly or unawares. I ask You to have them to free my soul from all bondage by whatever means is

EPILOGUE

required and I agree and say that the power of Jesus is all-powerful and effective to do this. Now, Father, I ask You to send Your angels to gather and restore to their proper place all the pieces of my fragmented mind, will, emotions, appetite, intellect, heart, personality, and subconscious mind, and bring them into proper positions perfectly as You planned them when You formed Adam and Eve in the garden of Eden. In the authority of Jesus, I break and cast out the power of all curses on my head and on my soul (my mind, will, and emotions). Father, I ask You to send angels to remove any part of another's soul from me and put it back into its rightful place within them, in Jesus' Name according to Psalm 23:3 ("He restores my soul…"). Now, Father, I offer up to You that part of my soul that has been replaced within me, and I ask You to cleanse it and sanctify it in Jesus' Name. Amen.

I encourage you to get around people that you want to be like. We are greatly influenced both by who and what we're surrounded by. Open your eyes to what goes on around you. Observe the people that you're with throughout the day. Are they a reflection of what you want to become? If not, begin to make some changes. Find people who are examples of what you would like to be in the future. Make it your goal to affect those around you instead of letting them affect you. Who you hang out with is most likely who you will become.

I recently found a quote from an unknown source that is truly inspiring to me. It said, "No one can go back and make a brand-new start…but anyone can start from here and make a brand-new end."[7] Even if your situation seems hopeless, with God's help, I can guarantee it's not. I've seen Him specialize in the things that seem to have no solution. Also, I encourage you to get all the help you can from local shelters. They specialize in directing you to the contacts you'll need to walk out the beginnings of a brand-new beginning that's free of abuse.

Here is a quote I like: "When I was young and free and my imagination had no limits, I dreamed of changing the world. As I grew older and wiser, I discovered the world would not change, so I shortened my sights somewhat and decided to change only my country. But it, too, seemed immovable. As I grew into my twilight years, in one last desperate attempt, I settled for changing only my family, those closest to me, but alas, they would have none of it. And now as I lie on my

EPILOGUE

deathbed, I suddenly realize: *If I had only changed myself first, then by example I would have changed my family. From their inspiration and encouragement, I would have been able to better my country and, who knows, I may have even changed the world*" (Anonymous, on the tomb of an Anglican Bishop, A.D. 1100, whose tomb is in Westminster Abbey in London, England).[8]

My prayer for you is that just as I allowed my precious Father to carry me out of an abusive situation, you will allow God to carry you out of your mess and bring you to Himself.

> *"...God says, '...I will round up all the hurt and homeless...I will transform the battered into a company of the elite. I will make a strong nation out of the long lost, a showcase exhibit of God's rule in action'..."*
> *(Micah 4: 6–7, MSG).*

My prayer is that you will allow Him to do what He so longs to do in you.

With much love and encouragement,

Rebecca

BREAKING IT DOWN

Abuse does not occur because two people disagree or argue. Rather, the bottom line to abuse, at least as I see it, is summed up in one word: control. I've heard others use the term "mistreatment." An abuser is someone who wants to control and maintain power by using fear. The abuser feels the need to be in control, and if left unchecked, he or she literally may become addicted to the power that it brings. This stems from an unhealthy need to feel important. Sometimes these men and women feel a need to be in leadership to prove their significance. Mistreating, or abusing, gives them a sense of power. Some studies say the abuser gets his or her sense of self-worth by abusing. No matter how you look at it, abuse is purposeful behavior that is bent on controlling someone. The abuser often is lonely and many times was a victim him or herself from childhood. He or she feels extremely inadequate and unfulfilled. To compensate for that, he or she feels that being in control of life or another person will meet that empty need.

Abusers have not matured socially, so they are unable to relate to other people with any type of feeling. As a result, they do not have a best friend to discuss deep, meaningful issues with—not even their spouses—so usually *no one* knows who they truly are. Deep inside they are still the abused child who is curled up in a fetal position and terrified of life. Since they have no sense of self-worth, they often are self-destructive. The outer display of confidence that is portrayed is a mask to keep the world from seeing their total lack of confidence, deep pain, and feelings of insignificance. Their actions speak loudly of their self-absorption.

Some common steps leading up to abuse and types of abuse are listed below. This is by no means an exhaustive list. I just have listed the things that took place in our marriage, in the order they took place. Things may play out differently for other people.

1. Charming—the abuser knows how to turn on the charm to "hook" a future victim. Then after the marriage or the two have moved in together, the abuser becomes

emotionally distant. This is communicating to the victim, "I've done everything to have you. Now that you're mine, I'll do whatever I want."

2. Isolation—the abuser causes the victim to cut ties with friends and family
3. Emotional/psychological/mental abuse
4. Neglect
5. Physical abuse (Please note that there is *not* always physical abuse present, yet all abuse still comes under the heading of "domestic violence.")
6. Stalking
7. Financial Abuse
8. Sexual abuse
9. Verbal abuse
10. Spiritual abuse—a term you may not hear anywhere else, but this is something that I endured

It should be noted that over time the abuse intensifies in frequency. The expectations may change daily. This is to keep the victim off-balance, as well as to reinforce power and maintain control.

In the following pages, you will find a brief definition for each type of abuse, listed alphabetically. This has been included for quick and easy reference. Just reading what follows will give you some understanding as to why victims have an incredibly hard time trusting. Again, these definitions and lists are by no means all-inclusive. Many other examples could have been given, but then the lists themselves would have become a book.

Much of the information below has been supplied by The Missouri Coalition Against Domestic and Sexual Violence. The examples have been written with the abuser as a male and the victim as a female to save time and space. Please note, however, that females have been known to abuse men, children, and other women. Men have been the abusers of women, other men, and children. The bottom line is if you recognize any of these symptoms, please get help for yourself or the victim(s) involved immediately. Please see the Resources section for phone numbers and other contact information. These organizations are waiting to help. The sooner you act, the more likely it is that one or more lives will be saved. It *is* possible to get free from all types of abuse and begin a brand-new life. If it were not so, this book never would have been written. Please

BREAKING IT DOWN

don't allow what has happened in your past to dictate your future.

Cyberbullying

This is any type of harassment made with an electronic device. It can include text messages or things shared while gaming online. Other names it can go by are online bullying, digital bullying, and cyber-harassment. In some states, there are laws on the books that will bring about jail time if the bully is convicted. The purpose of the perpetrator is no different than the bully on the playground: to control with fear, demean, tell lies about someone else, etc. (the list is endless). The end result for the victim can be suicide.

Cyberstalking

This is deliberate online, persistent, unsolicited contact by another person. It is potentially a crime in the United States. Laws are being put on the books in other countries as well. Stalking, in and of itself, is a crime. Cyberstalking is simply committed digitally.

Financial Abuse

Financial abuse is control over finances or failure to provide the basic needs of someone they are responsible for. Here are some examples. The abuser might:

- steal money
- damage property where she is living, causing her to be evicted
- destroy her valuable possessions
- cause financial debt
- ruin her credit rating
- control or restrict the victim in situations related to her employment or education
- cause the victim to lose or quit her job
- lose or quit his job
- control all the money
- refuse to work and make her support the family
- not allow money to be spent on her, the children, or her family—either for necessities or gifts
- make her solely in charge of paying bills while he spends irresponsibly (she has

to account for almost every penny spent)
- demand that the victim gives him the money she has earned or been given; he uses strong manipulation/ power/ control to get it
- spend money on himself that was to be used for bills or food

Incest

Incest is any kind of improper conduct between relatives. Sexual contact is not necessary for this to be defined as incest. The abuser, a sexual deviant, begins his purposeful behavior by grooming the potential victim. For example, if the target is a child, the abuser may begin by giving that child gifts. In the next step, the abuser will get the child to sit on his lap before he begins to place his hands on the child's thighs or buttocks, all the while building trust and the façade of a close relationship with the child. The abuser then places his hands closer to the genitals and follows this by moving on to exploration. Finally, the act of sex itself is forced upon the victim. From the beginning of the grooming process until sexual contact, several months may elapse. The demented abuser is aroused by the slowly increased activity and the anticipation of the next move. Each contact, however seemingly insignificant, feeds his warped desire. The abuse may even continue into the adulthood of the victim.

ISOLATION

An abuser is aware that if his victim befriends the right person, she will have the encouragement and resources to get away. To prevent this from happening, he usually tries early in the relationship to cut off his new partner from her friends and family. Also, the abuser may feel threatened if the possibility exists that the victim might gain financial independence, so he sees isolation as a solution. He may take drastic measures to ensure the victim's job is lost or he may prevent her from receiving job training or education. Some examples of how the abuser uses isolation follow. The abuser may control:

- where she goes
- how she gets there
- what she does
- who she sees
- who she talks to
- access to phone
- access to money

The abuser makes the excuse that it's because he "loves" her and is worried about her safety.

Neglect

Neglect can occur only when someone is dependent on another person. This usually applies to children or an older person, but it also could be a spouse or partner. Some of the things that could be neglected are:

- medical care
- healthful food
- clothes
- cleanliness
- shelter
- care
- love

He also might make her responsible for keeping the household running yet deny her the necessary money to do it.

Physical Abuse

The following actions all constitute physical abuse:
- hair pulling, scratching, biting, slapping, grabbing, spitting on, or poking
- shaking, shoving, pushing, hitting, restraining, or throwing her
- twisting, kicking, slapping, punching, choking, strangling, or burning the victim
- throwing objects at her
- any kind of touch that's done with control
- subjecting her to reckless driving
- pushing the victim out of the car
- locking her in or out of the house
- refusing to help when she's sick, injured, or pregnant
- withholding medication or treatment
- withholding food as punishment
- abusing her at mealtime, which disrupts her eating patterns and can result in malnutrition

- abusing her at night, which disrupts her sleeping patterns, and can result in sleep deprivation
- attacking her with weapons or even killing her
- inflicting pain with the purpose of intimidation
- forcefully threatening her, with or without weapons
- any intention to hurt or intimidate her
- locking up or confining the victim
- the abuser having unprotected sex with multiple partners
- excessive tickling
- taking the car keys away

Psychological Abuse

Psychological abuse is the same as mental and emotional abuse. It is used to wear down the victim's view of herself so she "admits" responsibility for the abuser's treatment. The bottom line: An abuser is a very insecure person. He is threatened at the thought of losing the one he has control over.

The abuser:
- is a master manipulator
- is argumentative with intent to intimidate
- breaks promises
- doesn't follow through on agreements
- remembers only if it's convenient for him
- creates tension in the home
- consistently avoids issues
- doesn't take a fair share of the responsibility
- harasses her as well as others
- verbally attacks, degrades, and humiliates his partner in private or public

- intimidates with a loud voice, destructive behavior, gestures, or a look
- blames her for his violent behavior to justify what he's done
- blames others for his problems and won't take responsibility for what he's done
- attacks her vulnerabilities, such as her language abilities, educational level, skills as a parent, religious and cultural beliefs, or physical appearance
- plays mind games, such as when he undercuts her sense of reality
- controls information given to the victim to alter her sense of reality
- attempts to confuse the thinking of his victim to keep her from resisting, gaslights
- tells her she's crazy or needs help
- questions her credibility
- behaves immaturely
- forces her to do degrading things
- ignores her feelings
- tells the victim how she should think and feel

- withholds approval or affection as punishment gives the silent treatment
- threatens to do bodily harm to her or others
- threatens to embarrass her, tell her secrets, take away her freedoms, or take the children
- regularly threatens to leave or tells her to leave
- threatens to kill himself
- minimizes abuse; he will downplay it, saying that it wasn't that bad, and will accuse her of exaggerating
- is unfaithful after committing to monogamy
- harasses her about affairs he imagines her to be having
- questions if the children are his
- stalks her
- always claims to be right
- causes isolation from her friends and family
- will take her to work and pick her up for total control or to show distrust

- will check up on the victim unexpectedly or repeatedly to intimidate her.
- makes her account for all of her time
- makes sure family and friends have uncomfortable visits
- punishes her when she arrives home late
- does not allow his victim to leave the house alone
- can be strongly manipulative to get his wishes fulfilled
- may force the victim to watch others be abused, including pets. This may not be understood as abuse, so it can result in psychological problems.
- destroys personal property
- accuses the victim
- brings up the past, but she's not allowed to; if she does, she's accused of being unforgiving.
- wants things to be done his way and only his way
- expects and/or demands that all of his wants and needs be fulfilled immediately

- demands a life of comfort for himself while those around him act as his servants
- makes the big decisions, little decisions, and everything in between
- handles the money the way he wants to, in fact, he usually controls it and is unhappy if she gets sick
- has an unpredictable mood
- gives "guilt gifts"
- downplays what she has accomplished, which shows insecurity
- purposely translates something incorrectly if she doesn't have a good understanding of English
- neglects medical care
- uses shame
- twists the truth by changing facts so he comes out appearing to be right when he was wrong
- uses circular reasoning

Sexual Abuse

Sexual abuse is usually very difficult for victims to talk about because of the sensitivity of the topic as well as how the abuse itself is carried out. This type of abuse stems from a desire to control. The abuser is afraid of losing control, even though deep down, he knows he is out of control. Sometimes the abuser truly thinks his victim wants it because it brings her pleasure. When there is sexual abuse of children, the abuser may prefer one gender over another or abuse both boys and girls.

Sexual violence or abuse can be indicated when the batterer:

- pressures her to have sex when she doesn't want to
- forces her to do sexual things against her will
- physically forces sex, which is rape
- is sexually violent
- has no concern about whether or not she wants to have sex
- pressures her to take part in a sex act that she isn't comfortable with punishes her if she doesn't comply

- uses sex as a weapon
- uses sex as a form of control
- uses inappropriate touch
- physically attacks the sexual parts of her body
- inflicts sex-specific injuries
- insists that she dresses more sexually than she wants to
- treats her like a sex object
- coerces sex by manipulation, sulking, anger, harassment, coercion, or threats
- is jealously angry and assumes she will have sex with anyone when that is not true
- is very possessive of her
- withholds sex and/or affection as punishment
- has double standards, such as has affairs, yet accuses her of being unfaithful
- calls her sexual names
- laughs at her or makes fun of her body parts
- uses verbal degradation during sex
- tells rude stories, uses rude gestures, or talks dirty

- denies the victim contraception or protection against sexually transmitted diseases
- forces photos or video to be taken
- goes too far sexually in public
- shares a photo or video without the person's consent
- engages in pornography or other exploitation
- forces her to have sex while she is sleeping or demands sex when she is ill or injured, after a beating, or soon after childbirth

Here are some statistics:
- 1 out of every 4 women has been sexually abused.
- 1 out of every 20 women has been sexually abused by her father.
- 1 out of every 50 men was sexually abused by his mother.

Often the abuser feels his victim deserves what he is doing to her. It may be that he was molested as a child. Often the abuser is trying to fix his father, past, or childhood through his actions.

BREAKING IT DOWN

Note that all this is planned and thought out by the abuser. His actions stem from a desire to control, and he is afraid of losing control. The abuser controls because he knows that at his core he is out of control. The victim, in turn, is overcome with guilt and feels responsible, as she often is told she aroused the abuser. Commonly, the victim can't shut her mind off at night, which explains why many victims cannot sleep.

> "One thing that surprised me was that, as the years went by, the more the sexual abuse troubled me. You would think it would be just the opposite, but that wasn't so. Time did not soften its blow. The more I began to comprehend just how much my sordid past had negatively affected my life and my family, the angrier I became with my abuser. Yet, because of my conditioning, and the lies my father had planted in my head years earlier, I didn't dare take my problem to anyone for help. My horrendous shame chained me to that silence. I think only another victim of incest can understand the amount of humiliation and emotional pain you feel after such degrading acts have been done to you—especially when the predator was your father. And my father,

being a minister, only added to my humiliation, for he was supposed to hold to a higher standard. That is why I refer to my incest experience as the ultimate betrayal… An important truth I finally came to understand is that when we harbor hate and hide hideous secrets, we allow ourselves to be continually victimized. *This greatly injures us, not our perpetrators.* They aren't even aware of our private torment, nor do they care. The mental torture and physical ailments that we receive from our private anguish only produce more suffering, causing our cycle of pain to continue."[9]

~ Shirley Jo Petersen

"I forgave my father, but I always insisted on having someone around me when I was with him. I did not feel safe around him even when he was 70, for he was not emotionally healthy. He was a psychopath. All sex offenders are, and they should not be trusted until a doctor tells you otherwise." [10]

~ Shirley Jo Petersen

BREAKING IT DOWN

SPIRITUAL ABUSE

> *Are you tired? Worn out? Burned out on religion? Come to Me. Get away with Me and you'll recover your life. I'll show you how to take a real rest. Walk with Me and work with Me—watch how I do it. Learn the unforced rhythms of grace. I won't lay anything heavy or ill-fitting on you. Keep company with Me and you'll learn to live freely and lightly.*
> *(Matthew 11:28-30 MSG)*

Spiritual abuse is imposing spiritual beliefs or values on another person and not allowing her to have her own. The abuser commonly uses those beliefs to enforce what he wants to be done. For example, he may emphasize that she needs to forgive, but he neglects his own need to repent and take responsibility for his actions. In *The Nature and Dynamics of Domestic Violence*, written by the Missouri Coalition Against Domestic and Sexual Violence, it says spiritual and religious abuse "manipulates her religious beliefs or spiritual values by, for example, refusing to allow her to attend church or spiritual gatherings or claiming that she is condemned and unwanted by her God or her congregation."[11]

Here are some examples of spiritual abuse. The abuser:

- says his beliefs are the only ones accepted in the home and no other opinions are allowed
- uses shame
- uses manipulation
- twists scriptures in an attempt to accomplish what he wants to be done
- can "preach" what he believes but doesn't live it
- exhibits pride instead of genuine humility
- gives the silent treatment to anyone disagreeing with his philosophy
- uses force when talking to anyone who disagrees with his philosophy
- twists the facts so he comes out looking as though he was right all along

- causes those who make mistakes to feel condemned and very guilty

- attacks, using intimidation to silence, if anyone confronts him with the truth of his behavior.

Stalking

Stalking is a mental assault. In all fifty states, it is a criminal offense to stalk another person. It is considered stalking when a person:

gives any unwanted attention that could be described as obsessive

- shows up outside a home or place of employment unexpectedly
- repeatedly follows, watches, or otherwise harasses someone else
- follows his victim through the use of a GPS (Global Positioning System)
- secretly watches his victim
- uses hidden cameras to watch his victim
- repeatedly contacts the victim or her work associates, friends, or family
- uses the internet to harass her, utilizes things such as social networking sites
- accuses her falsely or spreads rumors
- makes threats of any kind
- threatens to harm a victim, her family, or her pets

- damages possessions or property
- commits identity theft

- monitors the victim's phone calls
- monitors the victim's computer usage
- makes obscene phone calls
- sends obscene text messages
- solicits minors for sex
- consistently persecutes another person due to her ethnic background, religious beliefs, or political convictions
- sends abusive, anonymous letters, often maliciously sent to intimidate and scare the victim
- sends unwanted communication, such as letters, cards, gifts, emails, or other messages
- sends embarrassing gifts or cards, sometimes to her workplace
- goes through trash to find out information about the victim
- creates a situation where the victim needs to be rescued and then shows up to do just that

Verbal Abuse

> *O Lord, rescue me from evil people.*
> *Protect me from those who are violent,*
> *those who plot evil in their hearts and*
> *stir up trouble all day long.*
> *(Psalm 140:1–2 NLT)*

Verbal abuse is comprised of words and/or body language that are/is exercised to hurt, be cruel, degrade, criticize, or humiliate a person either in public or in private. This includes, but is not limited to name-calling, putdowns, and swearing. It often continues unchecked, never being recognized as abuse. Yet the longer it goes on, the more there is damage done to the self-esteem of the victim, and the more additional power is given to the abuser. When the abuser is confronted, he excuses himself by saying he was only joking. Another type of verbal abuse is withholding conversation, including appreciation or approval. More examples of verbal abuse are as follows. The abuser will:

- brainwash his victim
- tell the victim she is crazy

- blames her or others for his actions, gaslights
- minimize what she has accomplished
- call her names
- contradict what she says—this is one reason victims tend to be quiet and not state their opinions; they haven't been allowed to have any or have been belittled during the rare times that they have spoken up
- swear at her
- yell at her
- wake her up to yell at her and then not allow her to go back to sleep by continuing to yell or using some other method
- make demands of her
- use cruelty to control her
- threaten her, not only with his words but also with the tone of his voice
- mimic her speech or actions
- use sarcasm when talking to her
- cross-examine her
- ask her illogical questions
- threaten to take the children away from her

- deceive her
- turn something around that she has told him in confidence and use it against her
- turn her own words around to confuse her
- try to get her to feel guilty

Voyeurism

A familiar term is "peeping Tom". The voyeur gets sexual satisfaction from watching others when he is not participating or undetected. He may be observing the unsuspecting victim dressing, undressing, bathing, having sex with another person, looking at their genitals, or simply writing about something private.

Remember that with all of these examples, abuse is against the law.

Note: None of these definitions or lists are exhaustive.

FREE TO SOAR

ADDITIONAL RESOURCES

www.YourSaferPlace.org
Safe House App is available in Apple App Store and Google Play. This is a life-saving tool that includes a list of Safe Houses (shelters) by State, County, and City, Abuse, Military, Sex Assault, Suicide, Elder Abuse, Human Trafficking, and more! It's better to have it on your phone and never need it than to be in crisis and not have it.

Call 211 any time of the day or night for agencies that are available to help you with:
- emergency shelter
- disaster recovery
- food pantries
- daycare
- rent or utility payments
- elderly care
- mental health services
- employment
- volunteering
- health resources
- educational/vocational training
- emergency disabilities

- drug/alcohol rehabilitation
- domestic abuse
- counseling
- and much more

@freetosoar7987 the YouTube channel that informs about all things domestic violence; Co-produced by Rebecca Adams and Becky Vermeire

Flying Free Now by Natalie Hoffman
flyingfreenow.com

National Domestic Violence Hotline
www.ndvh.org
1.800.799.SAFE (7233)

National Coalition Against Domestic Violence
www.ncadv.org

Rape, Abuse, & Incest National Network
www.rainn.org

The Silent Seduction of Self-Talk by Shelly
www.daughtersofdestiny.org

Joy Bringer Ministries, Inc.

ADDITIONAL RESOURCES

http://www.joy-bringer-ministries.org/

The Whisper by Shirley Jo Petersen
Cedar Hill Publishing
Shirley Jo Petersen
1105 Sunset Lane Cadillac, MI 49601
whisperyoursecret@hotmail.com
www.healingprivatewounds.org

How to Rise Above Abuse by June Hunt
www.hopefortheheart.org
1.800.488.HOPE (4673)

Violence Among Us by Brenda Branson and Paula Silva

FOCUS Ministries, Inc.
www.focusministries1.org

Finding Home by Jim Daly

Stronger by Jim Daly

Caring for Sexually Abused Children by R. Timothy Kearney (Inter-Varsity Press)

FREE TO SOAR

All Grown Up and No Place to Go, Teenagers in Crisis by David Elkind (Perseus Books)

No Place to Cry: The Hurt and Healing of Sexual Abuse by Erwin W. Lutzer (Moody Publishers)

Through the Fire: Spiritual Restoration for Adult Victims of Childhood Sexual Abuse by Rick Meyer (Augsburg Fortress)

The Courage to Heal Workbook: For Women and Men Survivors of Child Sexual Abuse by Laura Davis (Harper-Collins)

On the Threshold of Hope: Opening the Door to Healing for Survivors of Sexual Abuse by Diane Mandt Langhem (Tyndale House)

Learning to Trust Again: A Young Woman's Journey of Healing from Sexual Abuse by Christa Sands (Discovery House Publishers)

Battlefield of the Mind by Joyce Meyer (Warner Faith)

ADDITIONAL RESOURCES

When Pigs Move In by Don Dickerman (Charisma House)

God Will Make a Way by Henry Cloud and John Townsend (Integrity Publishers)

Getting Rid of the Gorilla by Brian Jones

Stormie by Stormie Omartian

Beauty for Ashes by Joyce Meyer (Warner Faith)

No More Bullies by Frank Peretti (W Publishing Group, a division of Thomas Nelson, Inc.)

The Only Way Out is Through by Marte Tilton

Single Again and Secure in God's Love by Jim Smoke

Total Forgiveness by R. T. Kendall

A Framework for Understanding Poverty by Ruby K. Payne, Ph. D.

FREE TO SOAR

Divine by Karen Kingsbury (Tyndale Publishers)

The Penny by Joyce Meyer

Safe Haven by Nicholas Sparks

ADDITIONAL RESOURCES

Endnotes

Chapter One: Fleeing
1. Joyce Meyer, joycemeyer.org, *Good Morning, This Is God! Daily Calendar* (OK: Harrison House Inc., 2000), January 9th entry.

Chapter Two: Chaos
2. Shirley Jo Petersen, *The Whisper: Some Secrets Shouldn't Be Kept* (AZ: Cedar Hill Publishing, 2005), 63.
3. Shirley Jo Petersen, *The Whisper: Some Secrets Shouldn't Be Kept* (AZ: Cedar Hill Publishing, 2005), 65.

Chapter Four: Confusion
4. Shirley Jo Petersen, *The Whisper: Some Secrets Shouldn't Be Kept* (AZ: Cedar Hill Publishing, 2005), 149.

Chapter 10: Freedom!
5. Unknown.

Epilogue
6. Dr. Gary Wood, not published, used with permission.

7. Unknown.
8. Anonymous, on the tomb of an Anglican Bishop, A.D. 1100, whose tomb is in Westminster Abbey in London, England.

Breaking It Down

9. Shirley Jo Petersen, *The Whisper: Some Secrets Shouldn't Be Kept* (AZ: Cedar Hill Publishing, 2005), 58–59.
10. Shirley Jo Petersen, *The Whisper: Some Secrets Shouldn't Be Kept* (AZ: Cedar Hill Publishing, 2005), 218.
11. The Missouri Coalition Against Domestic and Sexual Violence, *A Framework for Understanding the Nature and Dynamics of Domestic Violence* (Missouri: 2006), 15.

Made in the USA
Middletown, DE
08 August 2024